W9-BXS-136

The Comic Spirit

Boccaccio to Thomas Mann

by Bernard N. Schilling

UNIVERSITY OF ROCHESTER

Giovanni Boccaccio, Charles Dickens,
Henry Fielding, Israel Zangwill,
Thomas Mann

WAYNE STATE UNIVERSITY PRESS, DETROIT, 1965

Published simultaneously in Canada
by Ambassador Books, Limited, Toronto, Ontario, Canada

Library of Congress Catalog Card Number 65–21652

Portions of the essays on Zangwill, herein, appeared originally in the introduction to the author's *The King of Schnorrers,* Shoe String Press (1953).

FOR SUSAN

Contents

Acknowledgments

Over years of study and enjoyment of the Comic Spirit, I have incurred personal obligations which I am now happy to acknowledge.

Let me begin with thanks to Kathrine Koller, who first suggested my line of inquiry, and to Ruth Adams who offered warm encouragement. Later the manuscript was read and improved by the criticism of other colleagues at Rochester: William H. Gilman, the late Hyam Plutzik, and especially R. J. Kaufmann whose support was indispensable throughout. At critical stages, I profited greatly from the editorial acuteness and learned commentary of my friends Louis Martz of Yale, Cecil Lang of Chicago, and Howard Schless of Columbia.

A number of my graduate students were good enough to let me test the work against their judgment, and I am grateful for the discerning aid of Donald Adam, Leo Rockas, Louis Dickens, and Joseph Pagano. But I shall never repay the joyous inspiration provided by my young friends who studied the Comic Spirit with me. I can only record sincere thanks to such prominent members of "The Drones" as William Dooley, James Falconer, Joseph Mack, and Peter Peirce.

Finally, I am obliged to Alfred Schwarz who was good enough to recommend the manuscript to Wayne State University Press. Here I fell happily under the influence of Harold Basilius and Ralph Busick, and am now the grateful beneficiary of their knowledge, experience, and generosity.

Rochester, N.Y. *Bernard N. Schilling*
March 19, 1965

Introduction

To a discerning man looking out upon the world, the varieties of human absurdity must appear endless. Seeing the many forms of vanity and hypocrisy; self-deception; unconscious violation of proper, sensible behavior; and on all sides the laughable incongruity between saying and doing—observing these things a man may respond in a number of ways. He may be indifferent, contemptuous, amused, or indignant, refusing to absolve mankind for its weak failure to be what it should be. Or he may think of himself as sharing like other men in the weakness that his intelligence perceives, and so end in a mood of tolerance—his laughter tempered by sympathy. He then sees life from both within and without, combining thought and feeling, discernment and tolerance.

The following essays offer examples of this way of seeing common weakness—the way of viewing the ludicrous sympathetically. There is no attempt at the wide scope of a representative survey here. If the reader asks why American literature is not represented, he may equally demand to know why there is nothing from French, Spanish, or Russian. The question brings in elements irrelevant to the purpose, emphasizing national features, asking wherein it is sympathetically comic, which alone matters. The examples do not represent countries or particular literatures as such: they begin and end on the continent of Europe more by accident than design. Although three different literatures are represented, this is not a formal study in comparative literature. If these are the best examples of a certain view of life, they must come from wherever the best examples are found—in this case, Italy, England, and Germany.

Similarly, this is not a series of studies in a special literary form or genre, although all of the examples come, as it happens, from prose fiction. No plays or stage comedies are studied, mainly to avoid raising questions which might be imposed by any certain form and its conventions. Prose fiction, however, offers the best chance for the free invention of character and for its placement in the widest variety of comic situations, seen from whatever position a writer may choose.

A chronological line is followed, not because this work professes to be a "history," but partly from convention and habit, partly from the easier view we can take of a given portrait as it seems to fall into its place in a recurring series—one that is bound to recur in writers of fiction with a strong comic sense.

The reader will notice that no special theory of the comic is put forward to the exclusion of any other. The reason simply is that no theory available is of any help in the present undertaking. Even Henri Bergson, whose *Laughter* has attained classical status among the endless speculations on the comic, sees "the facts slipping between the overwide meshes of the definition intended to retain them." The theory of the comic, blurred as it is by psychological analyses of laughter, remains one of the permanently unsolved problems of literary study. Douglas Bush once remarked, "As for Milton's syntax, it will not trouble those who leave it alone." On the ground that philosophic speculation will trouble rather than aid the present task, it is left alone.

If this collection is not a survey or a history, not formal comparative literature, not the study of one literary genre or comic theory, what is it? It is a series of illustrations of one of the attitudes possible for a discerning man, looking at some common forms of the ludicrous. The appreciation of Dickens and Mann do not profess to deal with their work as a whole, or even with the entire single books from which the readings are taken. They are here because of the presence of a sympathetic attitude toward the ludicrous in their work, Mann especially coming in as the last example, not only because *Buddenbrooks* displays great variety and range within the comic experience, but also because its discerning tolerance reaches a point beyond which it cannot go without becoming something else, without ceasing in fact to be comic and shading into the deepest pity and sorrow. *Buddenbrooks* may also be seen as resembling in its progression the movement of these studies as a whole.

Thus Boccaccio, Dickens, and Mann—beginning, middle, and end—appear in each other's company for no reason external to themselves. In these readings they see, but rarely condemn. To a medieval cleric who cannot keep his vows; to an indigent ne'er-do-well who cannot pay his debts; to the lazy schoolboy who cannot learn his lessons—to all of these they turn a similar countenance, more amused than angry—breaking at last into a silent, kindly smile.

Now the reader may still wish to know more clearly why these particular illustrations have been chosen, more precisely what he should look for and expect to find as he proceeds from one example to the next. It may be helpful to say first that I chose these because they appeal strongly to my own comic sense. The term "funny" is not critically respectable; it relies on personal response, and has no meaning to other than the individual who uses it. Yet to justify a certain choice among examples of the comic I must declare that these examples strike me as "funny." This is highly personal, but everyone's comic sense is his own and not that of someone else. The reader must therefore allow me to write my own work, not another's; he will then concede that my choices have to be my own. I must then evoke the reader's own response, until he is persuaded that my choices perform what they profess: to reveal the way of viewing the ludicrous sympathetically.

If this has yet an abstract air it may be helpful to explore in other terms the meaning which is given to it by the examples that follow. For convenience, let the reader keep in mind the terms humanism, discernment, and tolerance.

Bergson says that only human beings can be ridiculous, and study of the comic should convey a sense that human life is endlessly rich and fertile, inexhaustible in variety and interest. Yet if, as Fielding insists, comic insight lays bare the forms of deceit, human beings may be depressed and their lives impoverished by the loss of comforting illusions. Still, there is a consolation in knowing that men have a capacity for good sense. There must be a standard of some kind before there can be those contradictions of it in which absurdity so largely consists. Thus the comic asserts with Socrates that virtue is an objective reality known to all men who can see the ridiculous. If vice can be made funny, if hypocrisy is absurd, then there is such a thing as integrity. It is no accident that this is learned from Socrates, the ironist, or that irony should be marked in so great a lover of the rightness of things. A certain serenity for the reader should then emanate from these examples. It is wholesome for him to feel a kinship with what the comic reveals, to see himself as ridiculous when he is so, because if he is unable to realize that he also is vulnerable to human foibles he is not at one with his fellowman and thereby cannot share in the infinite enjoyment and variety and richness of human experience.

If only a human being can be ridiculous, however, he can be so only if he is also responsible.

Both comedy and tragedy assume that men have dignity and value, hence responsibility. Plato long ago argued the identity of the two great modes. In that magnificent closing scene of the *Symposium,* we find Socrates after a night of revelry, drinking, excitement, high argument, and the analysis of love; the incomparable instrument of God in the life of Athens is still on his feet, sonorously maintaining that tragedy and comedy are one, and going forth with undiminished power into the new day, searching everywhere for wisdom and virtue. Pope saw that human beings are ridiculous and great at once, that the more dignity and responsibility they have the greater is their potentiality to be absurd. This seems true even of satiric comedy, or the comedy of denunciation if you like. If men are not responsible for acting much better than they do, why bother to condemn, or to correct what is wrong? In tragedy once more man is great but is destroyed nevertheless. In comedy man is weak and small and inconsistent, but is redeemed by reminders of his greatness; his weakness is tolerated because he is man after all, and has what strength there is, within himself. If man is not great, then nothing is, comedy seems to be saying, although it deals in things which show man less than he should be. The comic humanist has great sympathy for children. Childhood alone is innocent, the only part of life not subject to judgment and therefore not open to ridicule. This is different from Wordsworth's view of childhood as a fading divinity; the child has just come from God, but the humanist loves the child as being the beginning of a man. A child is grown up when he is subject to being considered absurd instead of merely arousing pity or tenderness.

So comedy reserves its judgment until one is a man, only to hold one more responsible than tragedy does. The judgment seems directed at the individual; one appears more to blame for being ridiculous, since laughter condemns while sorrow commiserates. Here the theorists are certainly right about the corrective force of laughter. Tragedy seems to get at the common predicament and to show the individual man as tragic not only for what he is as a person but as a member of our species, doomed by the nature of things to sadness and defeat. But sympathetic comedy seems to alleviate the sorrow by emphasizing that each man has his share of a common fate. The individual's absurdity is accepted with the common lot; so as tragedy does not condemn, because a man's tragic fate is enough punishment, so the comedy of sympathy does not condemn because it is enough to show that the single man partakes of the general fate once more—and this alas, is to be often inadequate, foolish, inconsistent, incapable and hence absurd in the face of his acknowledged sense of responsibility.

Still, paradoxically, in tragedy man seems great after all, in comedy he seems little after all. It is not the grandeur of man and his possibilities that one sees in comedy, but the plain, the common, the human element levelling all into brotherhood. Before comedy can be sympathetic and tolerant, of course, there must be something to be sympathetic with or tolerant of, just as tragedy must leave something to admire. Comedy should be higher in general estimation than it is, but its emotion is bound to be tolerance and compassion, not pride or admiration.

If the comic experience is humane, calling forth a sense of the richness of life, willing participation in it, an acceptance of the full responsibility of being human, it also invites a certain discernment, an ability to see man as incongruously different from what he should be —a creature helpless before the needs of his body, weak, vain, and foolish when he might be greater in every way. The degree of this discernment in a man is often a reliable measure of his quality and stature. What a man discerns to be ludicrous reveals the extent of his intelligence, his wit and culture. He may go too far in judging what he sees, and so remove himself from the comic experience. It is difficult to be neutral if one is perceptive, and merely seeing that a thing is absurd requires appreciation on the part of the beholder, implying a whole list of assumptions as to what is passing through his mind.

But if this discernment shows others for what they are and shows in turn this man's own place in the human realm, it demands reconciliation between the man and what he laughs at as well. The reader will agree that for all of the acuteness, the penetration, the insight into men and things as they are shown by the five authors before him, they are all reconciled to their own membership in the race of men. In tragedy, my pity and terror come of seeing that the man who has gone down to defeat is myself; in comedy, as well, I cannot be separate from the absurdity that unfolds before me. I cannot therefore make too severe a judgment, nor feel aught of malice, contempt, or disdain. I must tolerate what I see with a measure of generosity, but if I should forget myself and fall into an excess of feeling, there is Meredith's remark, that the comic spirit "watches over sentimentalism with a birch-rod." This spirit is its own corrective, and if I go too far in any direction I become part of what comic discernment exists to correct—and it will correct any excess to which its own impulse may lead. I need only remember that if man is not great and valuable there is no case against him.

If my choices have been made then because they best illustrate the qualities of humanism, discernment, and tolerance, they are finally made because of their progression, their display of a form of tension that seems gradually to increase until the comic experience has passed into another realm. The detached amusement of Boccaccio is clearly far removed from the tender sympathy of Mann. Boccaccio has seemed the right beginning because of his assurance. His picture of surrender to a weakness of nature that harms no one leaves no doubt of Boccaccio's attitude. Nature itself is the hero, while institutions or codes that violate its freedom are left to adjust themselves as best they can.

In Fielding also nature is primary, although as a moralist he must take a position between right and wrong. But nature and goodness are cherished, allowed to prevail over a world in which they often seem absurd and which punishes them severely, but not favored in the end. What is vain, hypocritical, malicious, or mean-spirited may show great force, but it too at last becomes ridiculous. The tension of comic experience between seeing and tolerating here is allowed finally to resolve itself in a division simply between right and wrong. What is condemned emerges clearly as wrong, while nature and goodness command sympathy for all the ways in which they are weak in the eyes of the world, and command our moral approval as they are clearly right in the universal order.

The tension is most pronounced in Micawber and accounts for much of the difficulty acknowledged by students of Dickens in the interpretation of his character. Here the moral problem of right and wrong fuses in a single person, and the question is whether Micawber's absurd ineptitude expressed in harmless grandiloquence shades into cunning knavery that is bent on cheating the world and harming innocent people. But Dickens sees Micawber with affectionate sympathy. Those who insist that he is a "cadging scoundrel," in Orwell's phrase, must admit that he is a sinner who repents and makes restitution. But in that moment he ceases to be comic.

All three of the middle studies have much to do with money or the lack of it, how to deal with the world's demand for money when one has none. The Schnorrer manages to achieve an incongruous victory over this problem; the tension here is pronounced where the incongruity is so constantly present. Zangwill's success is to be measured by the degree of his persuasion, moving away from a sense of outrage at Manasseh's behavior toward admiration for his intellect and all of the qualities that make him superior to men above him in society and high in the world's esteem.

As the generosity of Boccaccio had seemed the right beginning, so does the pensive sadness of Thomas

Mann provide the final note. Mann's work likewise reflects in some degree the movement of these studies as a whole. As *Buddenbrooks* itself passes from the gay energy and fullness of its beginning to the dark tableau of its final page, so do its many richly comic experiences move gradually toward more sombre implications. Christian's exuberant nonsense, anecdotes, imitations, and youthful horseplay grow less amusing until they no longer serve to redeem the self-indulgent worthlessness of his personal life. Ridicule of Grünlich's appearance and manner yields to dismay at his scheming villainy. The absurdities of Permaneder and the laughable inconsistencies of the visiting clergy are lost in the gradual defeat and waste of Tony's life. And the comic exposure of school teachers in their unconscious pomp and vanity takes on a note of something dangerous or sinister as their gathering force combines to drive poor young Hanno out of the world. Hanno's own ineptitude before the demands of life has its comic moments but these are lost in the family's own decline. Mann calls forth then a compassion that is soon indistinguishable from mourning, and so moves beyond the range of the comic into another realm. Whether the comic and this other realm are in fact the same, counterparts of each other with the transition from one to the other being indistinguishable —this is another subject.

The Fat Abbot

Now there was a monastery in Lunigiana, abounding in monks and sanctity, that contained a fellow "whose vigor and lustiness neither fasts or vigils availed to mortify." It chanced one day that the young monk was going about alone toward noontide while the others were resting. The convent stood in a solitary place overlooking a field, where a well-formed country lass suddenly came into view. No sooner did the young man see her "than he was violently assailed by carnal appetite," Boccaccio gleefully making fun of the military analogy.

One thing leads to another until the transgressor manages to bring the lass to his cell "unperceived of any," in clear violation of St. Benedict's charges respecting guests. It further chanced that the abbot himself arose from slumber about this time and, passing by the cell in question, heard some unaccustomed noises. Coming stealthily up to the door to listen, he soon detected the presence of sin. At first the abbot thought to demand admittance, but returned to his own chamber to wait for the culprit. The latter, aware of shuffling in the corridor, "set his eye to a crevice and plainly saw the abbot stand hearkening unto him."

Boccaccio's protagonists are trained to think fast, having constantly to extricate themselves from desperate situations. Our young friend now tells the girl to stay quietly until his return. After locking the cell door, he goes to the abbot to give up his key before leaving the building; he still had to bring in some of the wood cut that morning.

This assures the abbot of a clear coast, but he does not know that the young monk has seen him listening outside the cell. His first duty would have been a swift exposure before all the other monks; but he thinks that perhaps the girl is related to someone who would not like having her put to shame, so he decides to see her first. Watching the abbot enter the cell, the lass begins to weep for fear of exposure, but the great man soon calms her disquiet. In a delightful passage of comic argument, the abbot persuades himself that there would be no harm in having some pleasure himself, now that God has sent him this lucky chance. No one would know about it, and a sin that's hidden being half forgiven, there is no reason for morbid and scrupulous rejection of a good that comes his way.

In short order the abbot is able to comfort the lass, who being herself "neither iron nor adamant" readily falls in with his purposes. The difficulties presented by the abbot's being enormously fat are overcome by a delicate and considerate accommodation, so that their consolation may go forward with entire success.

Meanwhile the young monk has not gone to the woods, but has stealthily applied his eye to the inevitable crevice through which he sees and hears all. Eventually the abbot returns to his chamber and sends for the malefactor, threatening to have him cast into prison, thus leaving himself free to enjoy the newly won prey. But the young monk subtly implies that all has been discovered, and while being very respectful as the *Rule of St. Benedict* demands, he manages to avoid punishment. He professes not to know St. Benedict's wishes in all respects and, to be sure, the abbot had not yet shown him how to make of women a means of self-abnegation: "But now that you have shown it me, I promise you, so you will pardon me this default, never again to offend therein, but still to do as I have seen you do." Clearly the abbot should not inflict a punishment which he has no less deserved himself. They both agree to say nothing, and after the girl is safely gone Boccaccio tells us "It is believed that they caused her return thither more than once thereafterward."

Boccaccio, shrewd and tolerant, will not lose his charm while the comic spirit is alert to men who say or promise one thing, and then actually do, in their weakness, something quite different. In the middle ages there was a universal ideal of behavior with a formal custodian, the church, telling men what they should profess. Yet it seemed that clearness of theory only invites transgression, and if a rule is one thing while practice is another the rule becomes an end in itself, giving a false security within which to indulge human feelings. A rule is less likely to be followed the higher it is aimed. The ordinary lines of behavior in Boccaccio's time were good enough for most men in and out of the monasteries and, as always, people were influenced mainly by example. When the ideal became content with its own statement and preservation, one might cease to worry over failures to practice it. The ideal might then pass to an institution, an order, or special set of rare persons able to sustain it.

In theory, the middle ages desired unity, agreement, control, and actual daily behavior might go its own way while avoiding scandal. This encouraged a degree of cynicism and hypocrisy whose only aim was to avoid scandal. Compromises had to be made, and inconsistent behavior was not transgression if not publicly known. St. Bonaventure held that it is more grievous to scandalize others than to sin in secret. Bishops were often more concerned to avoid scandal outside the monastery than to inflict punishment within. On the whole a certain generous wisdom prevailed and those unable to follow the standard could at least be discreet. It is reported that Albert the Magnificent, Archbishop of Hamburg, felt obliged to demand continence of his clergy, but if the strain proved too great they should at least try to live *si non caste, tamen caute,* if not chastely then cautiously.

We need hardly repeat here the dreary records of clerical misbehavior. The details are so common that we may easily follow Boccaccio's picture of the fat abbot and his lusty young monk. Yet we should keep in mind that he does not try to be irreverently funny about all the misdeeds of the clergy. Though he is sympathetic, as befits a great comic humanist, he makes clear the limitations upon his tolerance. He declares genuine reverence for the ideal to which some of the clergy adhered, and to the existence of which the hypocrisy of others testified. On the other hand, meanness, smallness, avarice, and hypocritical cunning are bad no matter where they occur and are seldom treated with patience.

Still, Boccaccio's sympathy is with our common nature, not with the gloom of an impossible ideal. This is the Renaissance in him, though his own age sensibly distinguished between the sins of nature, the merely carnal ones of gluttony, lechery, sloth, and the spiritual sins of pride, deliberate violence, or malice. His own humanism accepts reality and nature, taking people as they are. He is therefore amused by the fat abbot and the trouble he has justifying what he cannot help. He sees the abbot's mistake, not in eating and making love, but in belonging to an organization that requires what is impossible for him. The error is not in our humanity, but in denial of it.

A famous document, *The Rule of St. Benedict,* will tell us clearly how the abbot had promised to behave. Among the codes of behavior governing religious orders, that of St. Benedict was eventually adopted as more reasonable than any other. Benedict had come of an illustrious Roman family (c. 480–543 A.D.). While in his teens, however, he forsook worldly happiness and resided in a dark cave amid inaccessible hills. For three years he continued to battle against temptation, haunted by the memory of a beautiful creature whom he had once seen in Rome. Clearly he was the victim of a favorite devil's device: a woman whose presence either in person or as a vision must be combated by valiant means.

Once, in the twelfth century, a Spanish saint found the devil in his cell, taking the form of a lovely girl who sought refuge from her pursuers. The saint was obliged to sustain his resolution by branding himself with fire to the bone of his arm.

And the holy Godric of Wales at first tried rolling in thorns and brambles to subdue his fiery nature; then he buried a cask filled with water in the floor of his cell. At the onset of desire Godric would shut himself in this cask, varying the treatment by occasionally passing the night shut up to his chin in a river, of which he had broken the ice. Benedict, however, could avoid such an extreme. He mortified the senses by shedding his rude garments of animal skin and casting himself into a nearby clump of thorns and brambles. When his body was a mass of blood and wounds, he had once and for all routed temptation.

Benedict's fame soon attracted a number of disciples, thus irritating a wicked and envious priest of the neighborhood, who sought to undermine the influence of his rival. He caused to be introduced into a garden where the young monks were working a parcel of seven lewd and naked women who, by lascivious gesticulations and obscene postures, strove to tempt the disciples beyond resistance. Benedict saw that one disarms such an enemy only by retreat, and shortly withdrew from the region.

We seem to lean toward a military figure of speech for the spiritual progress of Benedict, and the *Rule* itself offers the same analogy between war and the religious life. The devil has simply declared war, as reported by John Milton in *Paradise Lost,* and eternal valor is the price of virtue on the battlefield. Under St. Benedict, one who joins a monastery is *militans sub regula vel abbate,* performing his military service under a rule or abbot. The analogy to warfare breaks down, however, since the best means of combat is retreat, already shown in Benedict's own practice.

St. Bonaventure also maintains that there is no real safety but in flight, in which he is supported by another guide to virtue, the Rev. Laurence Sterne. Yorick's *Sentimental Journey* has taken him to Paris where the devil appears in the form of "the fair fille de chambre." When resisted, the devil will take to his heels. "But I seldom resist him at all; from a terror, that though I may conquer, I may still get a hurt in the combat—So I give up the triumph for security; and instead of thinking to make him fly, I generally fly myself."

St. Benedict and Sterne are right. Before temptation, one has only three chances: to advance boldly and rout the enemy by a display of power; to bow down to forces greater than personal virtue, as is usually the case; or to make certain of victory in the paradox of headlong flight. If a virtuous life is like a battle it is one in which heroism flees. Yet the heroic coward carries with him as he runs away the thing from which he is fleeing.

The *Rule* is less paradoxical in other requirements. Of the standard monastic vows—poverty, chastity, and obedience—St. Benedict stresses obedience and poverty, while chastity is generally assumed. A monk must remain in the monastery till death and live obedient to the *Rule* which enumerates seventy-two "instruments of good works," with number fifty-nine offering a summary in the prohibition "not to fulfill the desires of the flesh; to hate one's own will." Little is said of relationships with the outside world. A monk, for example, is not to associate with guests in the monastery; he is to salute a stranger humbly, ask his blessing, and pass on. He is not to accept letters or tokens without the abbot's permission, and his life is ordered from end to end of every day. As "idleness is the enemy of the soul," time is entirely accounted for, although one may rest after the meal which follows the sixth hour. Further, the monastery is so constructed (clause sixty-six of the *Rule*) that it is self-contained, having all necessary things such as water, a mill, a bakery, a garden, and various crafts established within it. A monk is then to spend his life where temptation will never have a chance to assail his virtue. He abandons the outside world where the devil could assume his favorite image of female charm, and he does not converse with persons who come into the monastery from without.

St. Benedict describes the ideal abbot as well. He must be learned in the law of God, chaste, sober, and merciful; he must hate sin and love the brethren. He must give good example and be consistent in word and deed. His authority is absolute, but he must use it with mercy and discretion. The *Rule* does allow for the chance that an abbot may say one thing and do another, but he must be obeyed none the less, "even though he himself (which God forbid) should act otherwise."

A monk is also obliged to confess his sins to the abbot, so that the stealthy eavesdropping in Boccaccio was in theory unnecessary. In turn, the abbot's judgments should mingle gentleness with severity, giving him a wide discretion to consider the personal qualities of the offender and win him back to virtue.

These passages in the *Rule* come to mind as Boccaccio's abbot considers the problem of discipline; he is in keeping with the *Rule* until, alas, he is himself tempted. So also the young monk must not seem to reprove the abbot, which allows Boccaccio to set down one of those adroit circumlocutions of which he is a master.

But all commands turn upon this one: at the last judgment the abbot must give an account both of his teaching and the obedience of his disciples. If the monks do not obey he is at fault as implied in the sly remark of his young antagonist, that he will henceforth "do as I have seen you do." This places the abbot in a most awkward position; the *Rule* says, "While correcting others by his admonitions, he will be himself cured of his own defects." Thus he can be only half right if his own sin is concealed; he can correct the young monk, even though he does not cure his own defects. Yet the abbot must never forget the final safeguard against abuse of his enormous power.

With ludicrous effect Boccaccio's tale turns upon the abbot's knowledge that he must answer to God. If he can make it seem that God encourages his adventure with the girl, why not proceed? Hence the elaborate self-justification needed to get 'round the last obstacle in the abbot's way: God has to seem like an employer who would not have provided this chance unless it were to be accepted readily. So the *Rule* leads naturally into a story wherein the abbot must seem in harmony with his ideal at the very moment when he shows that he cannot live up to it.

This remarkable tale consumes hardly five pages, but we need many more to savor its delights and overtones. We learn a good deal about Boccaccio himself and his view of life from this and similar stories. It is true that his other Italian works deal more directly in his personal affairs; still the *Decameron* reveals a sunny and affirmative nature. The stories bear out his own statements of intention, his self-defense when he chooses to offer one. Boccaccio intends to laugh at absurdity, to rid the ladies in his audience of melancholy; he has no intention of reforming the age, certainly not in love or other impulses of nature. Love is a master of shifts and devices, a quickener of wit and invention, full of feints and subterfuges on the spur of the moment. Young lovers are constrained to commit sin, "if that can be called sin which young folk do for love." Indeed Boccaccio's main concern as a writer seems to be love in one form or another. Human needs are primary then, whereas artificial standards of conduct opposing them must yield to the force of nature.

Boccaccio's endless patience extends to the three characters in the story before us. Circumstances plus a certain frailty are too much for the resistance of the abbot, the young monk, or the well-favored lass. Their sins are not a defiance of God; the sinners only give way before luck and their own weakness, in each case so understandably human. Like other storytellers Boccaccio gives a large role to pure chance, and this too comes of his tolerant humanism. What happens for good or ill simply follows from the inexhaustible possibilities of life. The words "it chanced" recur all over the stories. "It chanced" that the young monk saw a buxom girl; "it chanced" that the abbot arose from sleep and passed by the monk's cell just when he was being most ardent. "It chanced" of course that Boccaccio himself had seen Fiammetta at a church service and so came under the main influence of his personal life. Luck is influential and people are weak; we must not blame them too severely.

So much reliance on luck makes for a certain artistic sloppiness, the author letting coincidence replace a thoughtful construction. But there are compensations; let us read again the passage where, in the space of two sentences, so much is made to happen. Despite the disunity of sentence and paragraph, there is a fine economy of means, a sense of abundance that helps achieve the comic effect:

> It chanced one day, toward noontide, when all the other monks slept, that, as he went all alone round about the convent, which stood in a very solitary place, he espied a very well-favored lass, belike some husbandman's daughter of the country, who went about the fields culling certain herbs, and no sooner had he set eyes on her than he was violently assailed by carnal appetite. Wherefore, accosting her, he entered into parley with her and so led on from one thing to another that he came to an accord with her and brought her to his cell, unperceived of any; but whilst, carried away by overmuch ardor,

> he disported himself with her less cautiously than was prudent, it chanced that the abbot arose from sleep and, softly passing by the monk's cell, heard the racket that the twain made together; whereupon he came stealthily up to the door to listen, that he might the better recognize the voices and, manifestly perceiving that there was a woman in the cell, was at first minded to cause open to him, but after bethought himself to hold another course in the matter and, returning to his chamber, awaited the monk's coming forth.

The narrative teems with life and experience. Boccaccio wastes no time, things are directly under way, and we respond to the sheer quantity of life that pours out upon the page. Boccaccio is limited only by the physical dimensions of his art. His material is constantly pressing against the confines of the art form used to convey it. Hence every line has to count and seize upon as much life as it will hold lest he fail to express a fraction of his immense discernment. He will summarize in a few sentences a mass of preliminaries or transitions to get on with the main event which follows logically from what has happened before. Most of his dialogue is also functional; it is seldom used only to reveal character, but is part of the action.

Boccaccio has a number of expressions for his impatience, especially when he has brought two lovers, his standard characters, to an understanding or "an accord." He will say, "There needed no more words . . ."; "Brief, he told him . . ."; "In brief . . ."; "Without making any more words. . . ." Like Shakespeare, Boccaccio is often in such a hurry that he forgets to determine whether his supporting material is convincing or not.

In the present story his economy is not costly, but rather quickens enjoyment as we become immediately involved with the young monk "whose vigor and lustiness neither fasts nor vigils availed to mortify." We cannot be sure whether this young fellow might not have overcome his vigor if he had really tried, whether indeed he has not ceased his exercises in mortification just before they might become effective. We hear nothing of his having plunged into the classical patch of thorns and brambles. He has not used a hot iron or spent the night in cold water. He is unable to resist when the devil brings up his heavy artillery, the actual person of a beautiful woman. So the young monk is "violently assailed by carnal appetite," and the familiar military language prepares us for the collapse of the weak defenses of human nature.

The numerous other metaphors for sex activity are not so crowded with associations from the thing being violated. Images of fertility or cultivation of the soil for sex are obvious enough in any writer. Boccaccio adds others from the harvest and milling, from navigation or travel, from horse racing, and the like. But the military figures of religion are best applied to men's weaknesses and their defeat by overwhelming forces. In the tenth story of the third day, Rustico wishes to make trial of his virtue and so does not send the girl Alibech away as he should have done; that is, he should have sought the safety of "flight" or separation from the tempting fact whatever its form. So "temptations tarried not to give battle to his powers of resistance and he, finding himself grossly deceived by these latter, turned tail, without awaiting many assaults, and confessed himself beaten."

As with our young monk, we get associations of the

church militant, of Christian soldiery in the Puritan tradition, of men fighting a cause under divine leadership, of an "enemy" of mankind, the devil and his forces or agents—of these assaulting men from without and being aided by human weakness from within, all expressed in the language of attack and defense, of flying from temptation or standing and fighting with special aid from above. These associations come to mind as Boccaccio speaks of his characters in a battle which they desire to lose while they must seem to struggle against the winning side.

Against the vigorous monk the winning side shows its power by an amiable compliance with what is bound to happen. Boccaccio uses the girl most artfully as a unifying principle. Just as in any tale of a woman and two men, the well-favored lass, partly because she is well-favored, shows an urgent human need. Boccaccio gives her nothing to say, but she controls all that happens, and is indeed the cause of transgression, of the need to satisfy one impulse and yet to seem obedient to an ideal whose validity her very existence seems to deny.

The story moves forward with her at every step and she is at once the prize for which the two men are contending, and the reason they are in a conflict, first with each other, then against a theoretical rule. From early surrender to her tearful alarm and shame on seeing the abbot, to her relieved acceptance of the solution to the abbot's physical problem, she brings out the qualities of the two men. She remains always fixed and the same, a steady quantity of nature itself to which they return; yet she adapts herself to circumstances fulfilling the story's aim. So the human sympathy of the tale depends on the element that does not change, that is, the girl, her role in nature and therefore in the lives of men. Like the other characters here, she has no personal name, but simply shows how the humanity and tolerance of the story are perfectly suited to Boccaccio's use of character and material.

The child of nature, lovely and submissive, must now enter the monk's cell without anyone's knowing that she is there. Like all stories of intrigue, the *Decameron* narratives rely on secrecy and concealment, essential devices when people are bent on doing what will be condemned if they do it openly. The need for secrecy exposes men who cannot live up to their professions, but who must seem to have virtue none the less. Boccaccio is fond of using convents or monasteries that are "famous for sanctity and religion," meaning more famous than sanctified. For the fame alone counts and, no matter what goes on, the outside report must be good: the actual sanctity may be in inverse ratio to the fame.

In the first story of the third day Masetto of Lamporecchio introduces himself into a convent of women, "very famous for sanctity." Pretending to be deaf and dumb, Masetto is employed to cultivate the ground—which becomes a ludicrous figure for his fantastic sexual exploits as one after the other of the inmates sees a chance for adventure without its ever being known. The first young nun reasons to her companion that Masetto is dumb and so she can safely enjoy him, "e'en if he would, he could not nor might tell it again." No matter what develops from Masetto's operations, "there will be a thousand ways for us of doing so that it shall never be known, provided we ourselves tell it not."

Boccaccio ridicules such evasions at two levels. He makes fun of the fear of scandal, the natural tendency of the orders to hush up irregularities on one hand, and of human inconsistency on the other. Clearly he has more sympathy for men than for institutional decorum; and throughout the stories he plays with endless schemes for concealment and secret operation. His lovers, clerical or other, must come together "without any else knowing aught thereof," "privily into her chamber," or "unperceived of any" as with our young monk and the girl. Someone has constantly to be hidden or introduced in some kind of container; there are others who need to find out what is going on and so eavesdrop or peek into or through whatever obstacles there are.

The result is an array of crevices, keyholes, doors, corridors, windows, apertures, or accidental cracks and fissures for observation or communication. People are hidden behind this or that, and under or in something else, and we meet an assortment of stairways, wainscots, hencoops, vats, and particularly chests in vast supply. Boccaccio gets some delightful effects through these myriad devices for concealment and therefore of discovery; at the same time he reaffirms the primacy of man's natural energy, which will assert itself against all artificial barriers.

In the second story of the ninth day, the inevitable chest is used to smuggle a man into a house in order to make love. Why does it seem so funny if a man is in the chest and funnier still if the man is a priest as he is in this case? Why is it absurd for him to be sneaking in like this, and even more absurd if the object of his love turns out to be an abbess? Comic elements emerge through the chest, the man, his being a priest, his sneaking in, his making love, and its being the abbess to whom love is made. So amusement increases with the contradiction between what is and what is professed.

If an impossible demand makes for concealment so does the concealment lead to much comic eavesdropping. A certain amount of this comes when authority is vigilant in seeing to the observance of the *Rule*. But once more the eavesdropping scenes in the story before us derive their fine absurdity from the difference between profession and action.

One of the most ludicrous spectacles in the *Decameron* shows the fat abbot leaning over outside the cell door and peeking in while the young monk puts his eye to a crevice on the inside to discover the presence of menacing authority. Later, when the abbot is within the cell, our culprit returns and "stealthily betook himself to a crevice, through which he both heard and saw all that the abbot said and did." There is some vicarious enjoyment in all such listening, as if to say that people are always interested in what others are doing and, if it is illegal, they do the next best thing to performing it themselves, thereby demonstrating that this is what everyone would do if he could. But in our story it is one more sign that in a world of concealment there has to be search and discovery as well, that there is sure to be hypocrisy when men are asked to live as it is not in their nature to live, that they are bound to do what they will, no matter what they profess, and if things cannot be done openly they will be done secretly at whatever expense to theory.

So when the abbot rises from his regular sleep in the early afternoon he becomes for us a rare symbol combining the incongruities of Boccaccio's comic world. How appropriate that we should meet the abbot just as he rises from slumber, for he brings to mind a couplet in the *Dunciad,* IV. The experiences of young gentlemen just returned from educational travel are being reported. Among many scenes and localities the "young Aeneas" had paid a visit

> To happy convents, bosom'd deep in vines
> Where slumber abbots, purple as their wines.

The couplet is full of the very suggestions carried by Boccaccio's abbot rising from sleep. The convents are happy, it would seem, through the laziness and self-indulgence of their inmates, not buried deep but bosomed in vines, seeing where flesh accumulates through surrender to good things from the earth. Inconsistency, contradiction, lazy inactivity are made to seem worse by Pope's artful alliteration on the letters "B" and "P." The similarity in sound mocks the difference between actual life and the abbot's vows, all carried further by the plural "wines" from a cellar with many varieties of an alluring texture, in place of a single wine for sacred use by an ecclesiastic who, lustily singing as in *Carmina Burana, "ego sum abbas Cucaniensis,"* has brought to his countenance the same color as the purple of his episcopal robes of office, no doubt thinking throughout the "blessed mutter of the mass" like Daudet's abbé in *Les Trois Messes Basses* of his turkey dinner to come, Stevenson's "mad abbot of misrule" indeed, as he sleeps away the long autumnal afternoons toward the slow growth of a fat bosom and wine-dark visage.

To Bergson, all fat men are in some measure comic, as persons embarrassed by their bodies. A fat man's body seems the main fact concerning him, instead of the higher faculties of his nature. He cannot get out of his body's way and, if he is Boccaccio's abbot, he cannot escape the dignity of his office which is contradicted by his huge body and purple face. His fatness then shows what a failure he is.

In turn his size would not be anywhere nearly so funny if he were not an abbot; he has violated not only the spirit of man, but his own distinction in the world, his religious vows and duties. The abbot is supposed to be poor, but he loves to eat and drink; he is supposed to be chaste, but he has as much need for, and capacity to make, love as anyone else; he is pledged to obedience and to give good example in conduct, but he feels like doing what he pleases once in a while. Alas, the abbot is simply an enlarged extension of our own sensuality, materialism, and self-assertion. His ideal contradicts our impulses, as if it were set up in order to oppose everything we naturally are. But his office gives the abbot another degree of falsity beyond what others can be charged with, much as we have in common with him. He is out of shape as a man and far more out of shape as a responsible religious leader who has taken upon his humanity obligations beyond his strength. Yet his generous inventor is not too severe. The abbot's fat becomes an invitation to be patient with our common needs. The fat violates what we are less than do the abbot's impossible promises to be poor, chaste, and obedient.

But life wishes to avoid penalty, despite occasional lapses. Many of Boccaccio's stories show the hero avoiding the consequences of an action through knavery, quickness of wit, or specious self-justification—discovering a reason for doing what he will do anyway. The hero, in concealing his behavior from others, tries to conceal the truth from himself as well. Here the abbot is not long in establishing proper excuses, Boccaccio ridicules medieval hair-splitting and devious evasion of the truth, yet in a marvelously typical passage he lets the abbot defend the coming surrender:

> The girl, seeing the abbot enter, was all aghast and fell a-weeping for fear of shame; but my lord abbot, casting his eyes upon her and seeing her young and handsome, old as he was, suddenly felt the pricks of the flesh no less importunate than his young monk had done and fell a-saying in himself, "Marry, why should I not take somewhat of pleasure, whenas I may, more by token that displeasance and annoy are still at hand, whenever I have a mind to them? This is a handsome wench and is here unknown of any in the world. If I can bring her to do my pleasure, I know not why I should not do it. Who will know it? No one will ever know it and a sin that's hidden is half forgiven. Maybe this chance will never occur again. I hold it great sense to avail ourselves of a good, whenas God the Lord sendeth us thereof."

As the abbot is so highly placed he has a special reason for hoping to cut his sin in half by concealing it. Chaucer has declared in the *Parson's Tale* that "ever the hyer that he is in ordre, the gretter is the synne." But more important is the proverb found in lists of Italian sayings to this day, "*Peccato celato, mezzo perdonato,*" showing the timelessness of the wisdom invoked over a sin that's hidden being half forgiven. The proverb is the abbot's human assertion against unnatural restraint by the *Rule*.

Boccaccio puts him back with the wisdom of long ages and, while he exposes a piece of chicanery, he seems to side in with the abbot's excuse; after all, he has a right to draw on the proverbial common humanity in which he shares. Proverbial action is supposed to be wise and sound, based on long experience and recognizable as true. So the use of an untruth, as if it were proverbial, in order to excuse an action which the doer knows to be wrong, has several levels of comic inconsistency and self-deception. Since one may justify an action by showing that it conforms to a proverb, one is free to make up a proverb in order to justify something that violates another principle.

Yet a proverb is a form only of human principle; the abbot needs rather the assurance that God, the creator and ruler responsible for everything, really intends that this chance for illicit love should have come the abbot's way. To be sure, our amiable hill of hypocrisy sets conveniently aside the notion that God has sent this chance to show adherence to the *Rule of St. Benedict,* and not to show that He does not mind a little secret indulgence. So God is made to approve the inevitable.

But the abbot is not a blasphemous cynic through whom Boccaccio chastises the clerical knavery of his time. He is merely weak, and he has a great deal of trouble in life; just this once, when no one will ever hear about it? So he begins to comfort the weeping girl who is amenable to this treatment, having expected shaming denunciation.

Here follows an amusing combination of images of gravity, power, dignity, size, and weight as Boccaccio arranges to have the abbot get 'round the difficulty of his enormous girth. Such notions of gravity seemed to delight the author himself and recall Chaucer's reference to his own size, "This were a poppet in an arm t'embrace." In his "Conclusion of the Author," Boccaccio slyly refers to his own weight, and assures his feminine readers ambiguously of his own delicacy as a lover. He has heard it objected that "It ill beseemeth a man of weight and gravity to have written thus. . . . I confess to being a man of weight and to have been often weighed in my time, wherefore speaking to those ladies who have not weighed me, I declare that I am not heavy; nay, I am so light that I abide like a nutgall in water."

The abbot is not light and he has to consider "the grave burden of his dignity and the girl's tender age" to make sure that he does not irk her "for overmuch heaviness." So we have the picture of the abbot making love as called for by his heaviness, which is slyly likened to the greatness of his office; as one would crush her physically, so the other would overwhelm her personally. Boccaccio thus achieves a comic ambivalence of delicacy and consideration while he makes so much of the abbot's office at the very time when all that it calls for is being forgotten. He lets the abbot generously demean his importance as set down in the *Rule of St. Benedict;* he lets him subordinate his physical weight and superiority of position as his natural impulse would call for. So in the moment of his indulgence the fat abbot behaves with the lordly generosity and largesse of his great office; this, alongside his present behavior, underlines in full measure the comic incongruity.

Boccaccio believes that his two sinners caused the well-formed lass to return "more than once thereafterward." Having cut his guilt in half by hiding it, the abbot probably made atonement by other good works and the conscientious performance of his duties according to the *Rule.* God would certainly forgive him, since He was everyday called upon to forgive far worse things. As Heinrich Heine said, that is God's special business. If He is the same God that Boccaccio loves to analyze, we may be sure that the abbot made peace with Him in the end.

Fielding's "Preface" *and* Joseph Andrews

Boccaccio's shrewd intelligence has seen the abbot for what he is but refuses to judge him severely. In Fielding the balance is yet more striking between intellect and compassion. Fielding is just as sympathetic as he is discerning, as much as inclined to speak for the victim as against the offender. He sees things as they are, but like his hero Lucian tries as much to affirm the virtuous and genuine as to expose their opposites.

This union animates Fielding's work so we need not pry into his own life to see why we should admire him for it. Still, there was heroic labor and suffering behind his sunny masterpieces. One thinks of Mozart—beset by trials and poverty, hounded by debt and reduced to the humiliating debasement of appeals to Puchberg, Mozart could write the most urbane and civilized music imaginable—his anguish and frustration only now and then implied in the subtle ambiguity of his music.

So Fielding's *Joseph Andrews* was the work of an afflicted man, its gayety and tolerance lighted by a clear intelligence and only its endless pity for men suggesting indescribable sorrow at the loss of an exquisite child and the continued illness of a beloved wife. *Tom Jones* emerged from an even more painful background, with Fielding in debt, harassed, cruelly overworked, obliged to marry the servant of his dead wife—in all ways ground down into the sordid realities of life, and yet able to create a work of genius, alive with energy and laughter. To the very end he could not be defeated and gives us the *Journal of a Voyage to Lisbon* while in a most "deplorable condition" as he says, with jaundice, dropsy, and asthma "altogether uniting their forces" to destroy his body become ghastly in its emaciation, yet to the last unable to extinguish his heroic love of life or to defeat a humanity in which energy, intelligence, and compassion all are one.

Whether or not Fielding's own sorrows account for his tenderness, it is certainly there. He is at once a part of and an influence upon a more generous tone in the comic spirit of his time. Hard satire changed gradually into more gentle humor; punishment gave way to kindliness, and Fielding, the last of those clear, undeceived Augustan intellects, none the less found himself more patient than angry. Let us recall the scene when the infant Tom Jones is found in Mr. Allworthy's bed. The baby is a fact of nature, a reality; there it is, helpless and appealing, innocent as yet—it must be taken in, accepted, like any other truth—dealt with for what it is. But as Mrs. Wilkins points out, the baby "stinks"; it is more unpleasant to accept, the more sensitive one is to such offensive realities. The stench makes the baby seem more real, increasing its natural demand that it be accepted for what it is on one hand, and cherished for its humanity and innocence on the other.

The note of compassion remains in Fielding's comic theory which finds the ridiculous mainly in affectation. Deceit is the enemy to be exposed, but the vain man, absurd as he is, seems more tolerable than the hypocrite.

Hypocrisy tries to conceal faults under the appearance of their opposite virtues. It is by far "the most cunning as well as malicious of all the vices that have ever corrupted the nature of man." A hypocrite is more ridiculous than a vain man, because it is a greater surprise to find anyone the exact reverse of what he pretends to be. Most offensive is the sanctified hypocrite who obscures the virtue of others, and Fielding warns against any faith in outward appearance, especially of holiness or gravity. The villainous Thwackum has "a great reputation for learning, religion and sobriety of manners," and reminds us of Boccaccio's "famous for sanctity and religion" in direct proportion to the absence thereof.

People are misled by what men say of themselves and what others say of them. A pretended virtue inherits the earth and brings on most of the great evils of life. The terms cheat, poison, malevolence, cursed disposition, "disgrace of human nature and bane of society" are heaped on "the generation of vipers" by Fielding as he draws heavily on the New Testament and the words of Christ. Here both the lawyer and the dramatist are in action. Everyone remarks how much of Fielding the playwright remains in the novels, and here he blends with the moralist in making people show what they are by what they do, no matter what they pretend to be. The lawyer too believed that by their fruits and works you should know them, with his abundant chance to see how much difference there was between moral principle, as announced in his day, and the actual behavior of men.

Genuine religion and virtue then are threatened by the mere appearance of them, and a hatred of the false demands an equal love of the true. A famous passage in *Tom Jones* asserts that "Both religion and virtue have received more real discredit from hypocrites than the wittiest profligates or infidels could ever cast upon them." There is no doubt that the ideal of virtue is natural, that goodness is right, because people try to seem to have virtue whether they are capable of it or not: hence all affectation. All pretense is comic and therefore underlines what is good, natural, and genuine. But even Fielding sees that it is not enough to be good —one must seem to be so as well. No matter how unreliable the appearance of things, people will base their judgment on it, and will thereby make the façade of life the more unreliable. The truth is that one may succeed merely by seeming good, but not merely by being good. The honest man's consolation is, however, that if he remains genuine and unaffected, he can never be ridiculous as Fielding understands the term.

The first sentence of *Joseph Andrews* reminds us that "Examples work more forcibly on the mind than precepts." We hear it said that the book got out of hand, that it does not follow the original intention or Fielding's own theory of the comic. Certainly Fielding has too much energy and love of life to be confined in any predetermined way. *Joseph Andrews* is not a sustained ridicule of *Pamela* although it begins and ends that way. It is not written entirely in the manner of Cervantes who is mentioned on the title page, although much of what happens to Parson Adams is bound to recall *Don Quixote*. Nor is it throughout a clear example of what the "Preface" calls for.

Some very funny things here are unconnected with the theory of affectation; even the people who are vain and hypocritical are often comic for other reasons, and Fielding's treatment of them does not always take the sympathetic line we have chosen to follow. Still the most amusing things in *Joseph Andrews* are those that

Fielding intended to be so, especially Books I and IV.

Let us then take Fielding at his word and look for the most ridiculous things in his picture of human deceptions and pretenses. This will lead in the end to Slipslop and Lady Booby, their vanity and hypocrisy.

Fielding's generosity was much tested by the success of Richardson's *Pamela, or Virtue Rewarded.* Austin Dobson speaks of its impact on Fielding in that its "strange conjunction of purity and precaution . . . was a thing unnatural, and a theme for inextinguishable Homeric laughter." He is often charged with starting to write a complete parody of *Pamela,* then abandoning it to develop the magnificent figure of Parson Adams. But *Joseph Andrews* is rather a contrast to Pamela; a parody of it was Fielding's *An Apology for the Life of Mrs. Shamela Andrews.* Here Pamela is a scheming slut in league with her mother and Mrs. Jewkes to get the best settlement possible in return for the calculated surrender of her "vartue."

Fielding sees from the very subtitle of Richardson's work, *Virtue Rewarded,* that its effect was to recommend a form of business calculation. The term *Rewarded* contradicts what it modifies—virtue is not its own reward, and if it is not, it can be pursued like any other material end. True, Fielding also rewards virtue, but Joseph gets only Fanny, illiterate and for all he had known penniless, instead of getting Lady Booby, the counterpart of what Pamela had achieved in landing Booby himself. Fielding rewards virtue only after showing what real virtue is and what a hard time it actually has in life, until it deserves anything good that happens.

In *Shamela,* at any rate, he spares nothing to show Pamela as she really is. The mispronounced "vartue" betrays that it is not really "virtue," but something only resembling it, passing for it, with special variations in this case. It has an air of abstract unreality too when the mother is told that Shamela and Mrs. Jewkes "sat down and talked about my vartue till dinner-time," and later on when "We talked of honourable designs till supper-time."

The result of discussion and foresight is to turn down Booby's first offer of only two-hundred-fifty pounds a year, "besides several other advantagious offers, as presents of money and other things." Shamela realizes that a much better bargain can be made by seeming to refuse to sell. "I thought once of making a little fortune by my person. I now intend to make a great one by my vartue."

With her mother's advice to guide her, Shamela marries Booby and then takes up her affair once more with Parson Williams, an ingenious fellow out of Boccaccio, who was fond of discoursing learnedly to Shamela, saying that "The flesh and the spirit were two distinct matters, which had not the least relation to each other." With the knot firmly tied, Shamela proceeds to spend Booby's money at the rate of a hundred pounds a day, saying with considerable logic, "It would be hard indeed, that a woman who marries a man only for his money, should be debarred from spending it."

Fielding's last chastisement of Pamela through Shamela shows how the whole clamorous celebration of her "vartue" had exasperated him: he makes her ashamed of the mother who had helped her to so "advantagious" a bargain.

In an essay on *The Knowledge of the Characters of Men* Fielding looks about for ways in which to test human character. Let a man's actions be observed with those closest to him: if he is a good son, father, brother, master, servant, or friend, he may be relied on. If not, he is pretending any goodness he shows. Fielding must have despised anyone to whom he assigns the crowning self-exposure of Shamela; she is made to tell her mother that "It will look horribly, for a lady of my quality and fashion, to own such a woman as you for my mother." They are to meet in private, the mother is not to claim the relationship, and she may count on a small allowance, perhaps be established in a little shop, as Parson Williams advises.

The exposure of Pamela continues less fiercely in *Joseph Andrews*. The comic inversion of ascribing female qualities to a man is the easiest for Fielding to establish when he makes Joseph assume his sister's virtue. Like dressing a man in woman's clothes, it lowers his dignity and makes him ridiculous. Joseph's name and his own reference to the Biblical temptation in Egypt establish the desired associations.

Fielding makes it all seem the more outlandish by a glowing description of Joseph's physical beauty; we cannot wonder that all the women in the book seem to desire Joseph, as all the men long for Fanny—in the end they receive each other on their merits. Joseph is a fine figure and clearly desirable. He is ready for what life has to offer, and should live it freely, naturally. Fielding seems to ask, could there be anything more absurd than Joseph's not yielding to any of these women if it suited him? Why does he refrain? His reasons contain the essential ridicule of Pamela, of her virtue for the fraud that it is, and of Richardson in general. Joseph has a natural reason for not giving way to Lady Booby, although like Tom Jones he has a strain of amiable weakness that might have overcome his resistance. The natural reason is that he loves Fanny herself.

An amusing side of the story is made the more delightful by abstract discussion, at the very bedside, of virtue, honor, delicacy, and similar irrelevancies at such a crisis. The fact that so much discussion takes place in the presence of bed is one of Fielding's sly efforts to make the whole thing ludicrous. Its prominence in *Joseph Andrews* is part of the ridicule of *Pamela;* there the action seems to show the main characters on, in, or moving toward bed a good share of the time; in fact, this is what Pamela has in mind, once she brings her operations under legitimate auspices. Bed seems to be more natural and spontaneously arrived at by Fielding's action, however; much time is spent in bed by Joseph and others who have to recover from the endless accidents and violent collisions of the story. But Lady Booby, as Joseph tells Pamela in one of the silly letters imitating her own, had "ordered me to sit down by her bedside, when she was naked in bed," and later on both Fanny and Slipslop have strange adventures in bed, not to mention the discovery of Betty with the ardent Mr. Tow-wouse *on* the bed. At Lady Booby's bedside Joseph's resolution is sustained mainly by two things: the example of his virtuous sister Pamela, and the sermons of Parson Adams.

Now Joseph does not give as his reason for resisting the older woman that he is already in love with a more beautiful younger one; neither to Lady Booby herself, Slipslop, nor in his letters to Pamela does he say this. It seems that Fielding's desire to ridicule the virtue of Pamela through Joseph's imitation of it leads him away from his portrait of Joseph—a wholesome, simple, natural lad. We are told that he resists "by keeping the excellent pattern of his sister's virtue before his eyes."

Joseph is pure then for the wrong reasons, as Pamela's

virtue was never more than a scheming device. It is the more outlandish when a man keeps himself pure and chaste comforted by innocence and virtue as Joseph says. If in Pamela herself it was only a pretense, in a man it would have no point whatever, even if he followed solely the advice of Parson Adams, and far less when he follows what had never existed at all. The absurd unreality is again compounded by recalling that Adams had found chastity as great a virtue in a man as in a woman.

Fielding's irony is never better: it is indeed just as great a virtue in one as in the other sex, largely nonexistent, pretended or imaginary, and certainly unnatural as it is. Further, what kind of virtue is it that rests upon sermons, advice, and the letters of Pamela? Are not these equally unreal and theoretical, offered for the wrong reasons or with the wrong end in view? If Joseph is to frustrate Lady Booby, surely the reason is that he loves someone else to whom he would prefer to make love. To appeal to virtue is only one more of the abstractions, theories, falsities, or denials of reality which are constantly being exposed and punished in the book. So also, when Joseph refuses to enter the coach after being robbed, beaten, and stripped naked he is fearful of offending the decency of the affected prude who shields her eyes with a fan.

Fielding again ridicules the nonsense of Pamela's virtue by saying that "it is the spotless example of the amiable Pamela" which had brought on these "mighty effects" in Joseph, along with the sermons of Adams which, though genuine, are just as far from reality. As for Pamela's example, since she is what she clearly is, Fielding underlines the absurdity of anything done under her influence, especially anything that is itself unnatural. Nothing can be what it seems if Pamela has inspired it.

There are some final thrusts at Pamela, notably Adams' rebuke to her and Booby for their unseemly levity in church. Pamela's virtue having accomplished its purpose, it can be forgotten; here the essential goodness of Adams works to expose the affectation of the Boobys. Adams would not be in church unless he thought it was a place for the serious worship of God. His rebuke shows that the Boobys are in church for quite other reasons, having no true concern for what they profess. Lucian's principle guides Fielding's whole treatment of Pamela: anyone who loudly and self-consciously professes anything will finally appear ridiculous.

The theme of affectation then as called for by the "Preface" lets Fielding expose very early in his tale some prime absurdities. Other comic experiences are scattered among the riches of the book, and set off the main theme. Fielding himself slyly reminds us that *Joseph Andrews* will repay close reading, that it is at times a difficult, subtle book. He makes good his advice that we read carefully, especially when profession clashes with reality. He exposes deftly the neurotic prude who cannot bear to have Joseph brought naked into the coach.

The whole episode carries an undertone of Biblical reference, with suggestions arising from Joseph's own name, the parallel of the Biblical temptation, his resistance to which has caused him to be banished out on the road to begin with, the good Samaritan context wherein Joseph is fallen among thieves, beaten, robbed, and left by the wayside, its accompanying demand for Christian behavior, and the crude indifference of those who seem to be asking once more, "Am I my brother's keeper?" The Biblical note continues in the exclamation of the prudish woman on hearing of a naked man in the ditch. "O J—sus!" cried the lady. "A naked man! Dear coachman, drive on and leave him." This suggests a number of ambiguities. In the light of his Good Samaritan parable, Jesus would not have agreed to this demand from one of his devout followers that the naked man be left to die alone. If she knew anything about Jesus or what his name implied, she would never invoke what is at best a pretentious delicacy with little real place in nature, and none in the face of so great a human need.

When poor Joseph is finally taken into the coach properly covered, a good deed is done for the wrong reasons, as suggested in the preposterous comments of the lawyer. It will be the best policy to save Joseph because if he should die they who last saw him alive might "be called to some account for his murder"; so he is to be saved not on his account but on theirs.

Fielding takes a number of thrusts at the selfish materialism of lawyers, their everlasting sensitiveness to action being brought against one, the recovery of damages, the principle that "every drop of my blood should convey an ounce of gold into my pocket," and the absurd assumption by Lawyer Scout to Lady Booby that Parson Adams will not go through with marrying Joseph and Fanny if he is not paid, for "His only objection is, doubtless, that he shall lose his fee." As for the laws of England, they are equally clear about their material interest. "The laws of this land are not so vulgar, to permit a mean fellow to contend with one of your ladyship's fortune." And the minute Justice Frolick hears "your ladyship's name," no further questions will be needed. Materialism, cynicism, social injustice emerge in Fielding's lawyers and judges, along with the ludicrous ignorance of the justice who was sure that Adams' beloved manuscript of Aeschylus was a collection of suspicious ciphers. Materialism and ignorance come through in the doctor who conceals his professional limitation to deal with Joseph's condition under a mist of vague and pompous terms, and so takes his place in the long series of comic doctors in literature.

Hard as Fielding is on professional quackery, he is more severe on practical jokers, with their self-conscious, defensive malice, which will cut men down in place of sustaining their dignity. The half-witted jokes played on Adams are dealt with at some length; some of these Fielding lists by number, to show how crudely mechanical they are—about as much gayety in them as arithmetic has. A chair is of course pulled out from under the parson; a plate of soup is overturned into his breeches; gin is put into his ale; a firecracker is exploded under him; he is tricked into falling into a tub of water; and eventually finds that his pocket has been picked of the half guinea he thought was still there.

These are merry, dextrous fellows indeed, a part of the cruel reality that poor Adams must collide with to his sorrow. Much lighter and funnier are the portraits of Mrs. Tow-wouse, Betty the chambermaid, and the obese domestic tyrant, Parson Trulliber. Mrs. Tow-wouse appropriately commands the Dragon Inn, suggested by her appearance.

When Fielding wishes to be graphic, he compares an object to something done by his friend Hogarth; and after dealing with the person and voice of this creature, he is able to say "that Hogarth himself never gave more expression to a picture." Everything about her is sharp, peaked, bony, strident, in keeping with a nature in the last degree uncharitable, selfish, and avaricious. She comes more alive than Peter Pounce, a vain, hypocritical, grasping, usurious scoundrel, full of snobbery, pretense and justification for his cruelty and avarice. Mrs. Tow-wouse delivers herself of a number of speeches whose violence, exaggeration, ill-temper, and obscenity show her the special victim of the deadly sins of covetousness and anger in particular, having none of the qualities associated with Jesus Christ.

Her Christianity emerges only when it seems that "a gentleman" has come to the inn, and not one of the "vagabonds" she so detests—Christianity being invoked in direct ratio to the likelihood that the bill will be paid. Joseph seems to call up the compassion of Mr. Tow-wouse and of Betty, but to the lady herself he is a naked vagabond, and if Betty dares to touch a shirt to clothe him with, "I'll throw the chamberpot at your head." That Joseph is a poor wretch simply invites the question "What the devil have we to do with poor wretches?" Fielding thereby once more reminding us of the question of Cain. And Mrs. Tow-wouse does not improve the language by whose tone and quality Fielding asks us to judge her when she utters her famous comment on charity. Her pathetic husband suggests that common charity demands help to Joseph even if it is not clear how he is to pay his reckoning at the inn.

"Common charity, a f - - t," says she; "common charity teaches us to provide for ourselves, and our families; and I and mine won't be ruined by your charity, I assure you."

The surgeon's fear that Joseph may yet die of his wounds inspires only the reciprocal fear that "We are like to have a funeral at our own expense."

But Mrs. Tow-wouse's vocabulary and what it tells us of her quality as a person becomes even more graphic when she discovers her husband and the obliging Betty in an act of mutual consolation. Poor Betty is the object of a tirade of unmitigated fierceness in which the terms slut, trollop, huzzy, whore, and bitch are freely used, which last Fielding himself abbreviates with customary delicacy "to avoid offense."

Yet as Betty quite rightly says, "I have done nothing that's unnatural." And she seems on the whole to have Fielding's approval. She had "good-nature, generosity, and compassion," and her heart is moved by the sufferings of the wounded Joseph to whom she behaves with a charity her profane mistress was incapable of. Alas, however, Betty's receptive nature was too relaxed and natural, and what she tends to think about when performing her duties prepares us for her exposure to Mrs. Tow-wouse. On returning from her charitable office to Joseph, Betty reports she believed "He was a gentleman, for she never saw a finer skin in her life."

It follows that, with Joseph recovered, his physical attractions become too much for Betty's naturalness, and Fielding again presents us with the preposterous inversion of an assault on male chastity. On a "fatal evening" Betty is warming Joseph's bed and is unable to contain her impulses "after many fruitless hints and sly insinuations" probably much like those offered also in vain by the amorous Lady Booby. At last she throws down the warming pan, "and embracing him with great eagerness, swore he was the handsomest creature she had ever seen."

Let it be said to Joseph's credit that he is torn between nature and the twofold influence no doubt of his sister Pamela's virtue and the sermons of Parson

Adams. Tom Jones would not so have fled from his natural inclinations, but Joseph is obliged to be violent in thrusting Betty from the room and locking the door. If the novel requires any further exposure of the nonsense in Pamela's virtuous example—or indeed of the absurdity in pretending that the relationship between the sexes is other than nature intends—it would emerge in the irony of Fielding's comment on this new temptation scene:

> How ought man to rejoice, that his chastity is always in his own power; that if he hath sufficient strength of mind, he hath always a competent strength of body to defend himself, and cannot, like a poor weak woman, be ravished against his will!

Meanwhile over the years some change had taken place in the sentiments of Mr. Tow-wouse toward his wife, and he had begun to notice the inviting charms of Betty, going so far as to say and do tender things to her, "For as the violence of his passion had considerably abated to Mrs. Tow-wouse; so like water, which is stopped from its usual current in one place, it naturally sought a vent in another." Now poor Betty is in a desperate mood of frustration after being repulsed by Joseph, and for a while meditates killing herself. Here follows a delightful anticipation of that last poetic word on suicide, Dorothy Parker's *Resumé*. She finds that there is some objection to razors, rivers, acids, drugs, and guns, while "Nooses give" and "Gas smells awful," so "You might as well live."

For Betty now too, death "happily" came forward "in so many shapes of drowning, hanging, poisoning, that her distracted mind could resolve on none." Resuming her duties as chambermaid, Betty repairs to Mr. Tow-wouse's room to make the bed. Seeing him there, she tries to leave but he detains her with much tenderness and the whisper of such soft things, that "the vanquished fair one" ends in quiet submission to her master's will. Whereupon "Mrs. Tow-wouse unexpectedly entered the room" and delivered herself in the terms already reported. With a few deft strokes Fielding sketches in the lifetime of tyrannical abuse that lies before poor Tow-wouse, who must bear reminders of this transgression "once or twice a day, during the residue of his life."

The portraits of Barnabas and Trulliber carry forward the general theme of suspicion of anyone who achieves the reputation of goodness in a marked degree. Barnabas is concerned to pray with and over Joseph according to his formulas, so much is said of grace, prayer, faith, forgiveness of the thieves, looking to Heaven, justice, and the like, while Barnabas is thinking of the bowl of punch under way below. In turn when we know that Trulliber is "famous for sanctity and religion" and charity, we can be sure that Adams' naive appeal for help will get the reception it does, symbolized by his fall into the mud of Trulliber's pigsty.

Adams does not know that we must never judge people by what others say of them or by what they say of themselves. Trulliber is a vulgar, tyrannical boor who nevertheless considers himself God almighty. The arrogant abuse of his wife continues throughout Adams' visit, and nothing suggests his vain brutality so well as his not even calling her by a name of any kind, but merely crying out "Silence, woman" when she tries to support his repudiation of Adams. Trulliber's pious mouthings are an end in themselves once Adams suggests a loan and actually invokes the Christian ideal, to which Trulliber has professed such fervent allegiance. He is of course angrily, ignominiously, and absurdly driven forth.

To all such vain pretense Adams is himself a contrast, the noblest, kindest, best of men. We may well ask what role the most genuine of men should play in a book aimed at the ridicule of affectation. But Adams is not an afterthought, a stroke of creative genius that got out of hand so as to take over the main role in a novel which had begun with quite different intentions. Not only is he amusing himself in a score of ways, his virtue is required to show what the affectations of others are not. Pretense is better ridiculed against a fine example of its opposite; if for no other reason Fielding needs Adams to expose Lady Booby.

Adams fulfills the ideal of Christian goodness and learning demanded by his profession. He believes in good works and, simple fellow that he is, he tries to carry out his preaching. Unlike the absurd cleric, the "puffed-up empty human bladder, strutting in princely robes" who looks down upon his parishioners, Adams tries to observe Christian charity, to convey the virtues of piety and humility to his flock, and to deserve the opinion of Joseph and Fanny who are sure that he is "the best creature living."

But this very genuineness makes Adams seem dangerous to other members of his profession. His reprimand of the Boobys takes place in church and, as Fielding says, "our parson would have done no less to the highest prince on earth," disdaining all pretense, social and spiritual. Church is the center both of goodness and its affectation; going there is a concrete sign of virtue which everyone must seem to have; but only a few like Adams possess it and he will not have persons compound their hypocrisy in the very house of God. Ideals of conduct are hard to achieve, yet those who are supposed to be capable of them must seem to be so, or stand discredited. A truly honest man is terrifying among people to whose interest it is to seem something that they are not.

And so for his spiritual pains, Adams appears as dangerous as the devil himself to his colleague Barnabas. A consistent devotion to original Christianity, Swift had reminded the world, would bring on a complete revolution. Adams is a dangerous fellow who would follow the Bible literally; he would have the clergy poor and devout and would "reduce us to the example of the primitive ages, forsooth!"

Repudiated as a traitor to their cause by his clerical associates, Adams cannot expect much in the way of worldly interest. Fielding's *Essay on Nothing* concluded that nothing was what the virtuous, wise, and learned among men could expect for their qualities; so Adams' goodness suffers from reality by what it offers him in payment. If he will insist on doing his duty with no regard for his worldly interest, Adams must take in return the "handsome income" of twenty-three pounds a year for his wife and six children, generously conferred upon him by a bishop. He seems to be one of the items in Fielding's *Modern Glossary: "Fool.*—A complex idea, compounded of poverty, honesty, piety, and simplicity."

Clearly Fielding does not ridicule the clergy as such by his portrait of Adams and his mean condition. His "Preface" underlines the words "*no man can possibly have a greater respect*" for gentlemen of Adams' cloth so long as they are worthy. The important fact about

Adams' calling is that he is low and underpaid in it, showing that affluent clerics are not like him but ought to be more so. The difference in position and payment shows the difference in consistent pursuit of a common ideal, suggests indeed that the more elevated a profession is supposed to be, the less likely it is to reward or recognize those who actually perform what it demands. With virtue and learning of the highest kind, Adams is not much above the domestic servants, Fanny and Joseph, who are his real friends and who love him devotedly. So once more the signs of a real devotion to an ideal will be sought most by those least able to live up to it; since they cannot attain it, all the more reason to get the external rewards of having done so, as these will make it seem as if they have done what they are incapable of.

If the goodness of Adams has profited him little, his remarkable learning also clashes with the way things are. Adams knows a great deal after many years of study, knows in fact more than most people in universities. Though it is true that as a teacher his first concern is moral—he would rather have a boy "a blockhead than an atheist or a presbyterian"—he has a magnificent command of Greek and has often lamented that his wife did not understand this tongue. He feels that knowledge of men is to be gained only from books—"The only way of travelling by which any knowledge is to be acquired." Adams can offer no higher praise to the tradesman than this—he is a highly valuable member of society "and perhaps, inferior to none but the man of learning."

But, according to the Abbé Bellegarde, Chesterfield, and others, learned men often fail of that politeness which comes only from commerce in the world; when they leave their studies, the Abbé says, "Every step they make exposes them to the laughter of persons of less capacities." Certainly the absent-mindedness and crudity of Adams illustrate all that the theorists of politeness have shown to be ill-advised in men's behavior. But Fielding's *Essay on Conversation* maintains that anyone who cultivates the happiness and ease of others, however low his rank "or however clumsy he may be in figure or demeanour, hath, in the truest sense of the word, a claim to good-breeding."

Fielding loves and understands Adams well; yet "we live in a world of common men," not of philosophers or other odd people who are above the concerns of the majority. "We are therefore to adapt our behaviour to the opinion of the generality of mankind, and not to that of a few odd fellows." And Adams is odd—ignorant of the ways of the world as a newborn infant, completely innocent and unsuspecting. Fielding admits that forms and ceremonies have no real substance, but they are more important than they seem. They are in fact the only outward difference between one man and another, so they are expected by all civilized people. One becomes ludicrous if he fails to respect them. By so much is Fielding on the side of the world and custom, and he lets Adams pay for his eccentricities as Don Quixote does through numerous collisions, beatings, and violent accidents.

Here the title page is made good, and *Joseph Andrews* is written in the manner of Cervantes. It recalls *Don Quixote* in the physical collisions, the wanderings from one inn to another on horseback, and other like situations. But anyone who writes to show the contrast between what is assumed, pretended, or imagined and what is real writes in Cervantes' manner as far as it goes. Unlike the Don, to be sure, Adams is not insane, but whenever he is about to collide violently with reality his utterance seems to become more elevated, and his talk grows verbose, platitudinous, synthetic. The more sonorous and extreme it is, the more likely that reality will contradict it.

When Adams responds to the liberal gentleman's purely imaginary generosity at the inn, he talks with just the right degree of excessive affirmation to underline how far it all is from the fact. And when Fielding exposes the gentleman's promises next day, the medical note cannot have been an accident in realism. The gentleman had to send word that unhappily he could not lend them any horses after all, " for that his groom had, unknown to him, put his whole stable under a course of physic." And this from the man whom Adams would have "taken a pilgrimage to the Holy Land" in order to behold.

Examples of Cervantes' comic snowball abound for poor Adams too. Perhaps the most famous of these starts from the surly, ill-mannered host at the inn who gets into a fierce quarrel with Joseph and Adams: bloody noses are exchanged, the antagonists knock each other down, a pan of hog's blood is discharged by the hostess into the parson's face, Mrs. Slipslop herself enters the fray with much pulling of hair, cuffs in the face, and disturbance to the general dignity before peace is restored.

But physical violence, sharp reminder that it is, does not force the realities of life upon the unsuspecting so unmercifully as the need for money. Like Don Quixote again, Adams has a dreadful time paying the bills that seem always to mount up along the way. Upon Joseph's recovery from a leg injury, they are ready to move on when, as Fielding slyly puts it, "an accident a little retarded them," the "accident" being the bill for seven shillings. Nothing could be less of an accident than having to pay for one's accommodation. Yet it turns out that no money is on hand, since "The fellow who had taken poor Fanny's purse had unluckily forgot to return it."

Fielding with delightful precision prints the account as it would be totalled if the bill itself were to deduct the contents of all three of the travelers' pockets. A balance of six shillings five-and-one-half pence is still owing therefore, and they are reminded that nothing is so starkly real, so relentless and unavoidable, as an itemized bill. Fielding once more intensifies the reality and its consequences by having Adams jubilantly discover a well-to-do clergyman nearby, his "brother" who would certainly lend them what money they might need. He then goes to wait upon the odious Trulliber, with what result we know.

But Adams has many other amiable weaknesses allied to his own vanity and inconsistency, not to speak of absent-mindedness. This strikes us from his very appearance. Clearly Adams simply does not *see* what other people have on or what they look like; he makes no comparison with himself and so does not realize the difference between normal attire and his own outlandish costume.

He looks comical enough by day with a short coat over his cassock, and a nightcap drawn over his wig, but at night when obliged to rise in a hurry he appears without breeches, garters, or stockings, with a red spotted handkerchief over his wig, wearing his greatcoat over the torn cassock on top of some not very white linen, and so on.

Then Adams is continually ignoring what he should have remembered. He at various times forgets his hat, his breeches, his greatcoat; he forgets to pay right and left, and his inability to see through people and their operations is simply another aspect of an absent-mindedness that collides with reality. If it is dark and Adams has to be careful where he goes, his foot naturally slips, he falls and rolls clumsily to the bottom of the hill. We can be sure at the outset of the "ride and tie" arrangement that it has no chance to work, for Adams is bound to fall "into a contemplation on a passage in Aeschylus" which will make him forget his fellow traveler. Anything that has to be recalled, agreed upon with a complication of any kind, is bound to be fumbled. The horse is forgotten, Adams wanders off by himself, turns the wrong way, and is lost on the downs. This wrong turn has somewhat less alarming consequences than another that Adams falls into later on when, on returning from the encounter at Slipslop's room, he turns to the left instead of to the right and spends the remainder of the night in bed with Fanny.

One lapse of memory was more trying than any other: Adams had forgotten to bring along his sermons. This was remarkable, for he loved to give abstract harangues to anyone who would listen. He never travels without a sermon he says, "for fear of what may happen," and is always ready to assuage the anguish of his friends in their numerous crises with a pious discourse. Perhaps this readiness with sermons gratis and extempore made it seem needless to recall the vast manuscript, whose publication was in fact the whole reason for going to London.

The entire episode of the forgotten sermons shows Fielding's kindly ironic genius at its best as he pictures the amiable helplessness of Adams to conduct the simplest transaction in terms of reality. The irony begins when the sermons are thought of as a means of getting money on loan from Mr. Tow-wouse, money being throughout a symbol of that material advantage, return, or security which Adams like Micawber for other reasons was incapable of getting for himself. Now he informs Tow-wouse that he would like to borrow three guineas, giving for a pledge one of the nine volumes of manuscript sermons which were in his saddlebag, the whole being worth at least a hundred pounds. The sermons are delightfully built up for the anticlimax of Adams' having forgotten them, and what we know all along to be their worthlessness in money is underlined by their nonexistence, and indeed corresponds to it.

Adams' colleague, Mr. Barnabas, a pretentious ignoramus full of voluble suggestions, introduces him to a man who he said was a bookseller "and would be as likely to deal with him for his sermons as any man whatever." This delightful ambiguity is lost on Adams, who proceeds to his business negotiation with hopeless naivete, disclosing his dire need of getting money for them now, offering to read some as a specimen, and avowing with pitiful simplicity that an honest mind ought to be more willing to lose money through good sermons than to make profit from bad ones. Alas, he was dealing with a commercial publisher, one of a group of men noted to this day for the austerity of their realism. It turns out that the sermons would not sell, and it was the publisher's opinion that those persons, who gain by preaching sermons, "are the properest to lose by printing them." Even if Adams had remembered to bring what he had set out to dispose of, the manuscript would have been of no value. It seems that Mrs. Adams had put in shirts, shoes, and other necessaries, quite rightly assuming, even though he was going away in order to sell his sermons, that her husband would "want shirts more than sermons on his journey," certainly more than these particular sermons. Fielding delights us with an inverted absent-mindedness here, for Adams hasn't really forgotten anything after all; he has simply gone away without that which would have been of no value even if he had remembered to bring it.

Adams is much put out later on when he fumbles vainly in his pockets, searching for the masterpiece among his sermons. This was a discourse on vanity; Adams declares that he has never been a greater enemy to any human passion than to vanity. And here Fielding brings even his most-beloved friend in line with the "Preface." It is easy to laugh all along at Adams' eccentricities and little weaknesses, his snoring like an ass's bray, his absurd belief in witchcraft, ghosts, and spirits, his jumping about, dancing and snapping his fingers when excited—all these are as harmless as his little vanities. It is often remarked how vain he was of his sermons, how well he thought he knew the world of men, and how proud he was of the schoolmasters of the world and his own eminence among them, his being "second to none" as a teacher.

More comic is the vanity of his supposing that he was a very logical character, but he was of course too absent-minded to see how contradictory he was. Preaching submission to God's will, and the need of resignation like the philosopher in *Rasselas,* Adams is plunged into agonies of despair by a false report of the drowning of one of his children. But he has no trouble changing his mood to lyrical happiness when the child is recovered, never thinking that he has contradicted himself. He decries physical pleasure, yet consumes lakes of ale, beer, and punch, eats prodigiously, and smokes until his very person is saturated with the odor of tobacco. He preaches the control of passion and emotion, but rushes from one extreme to another. He disapproves of angry disputes but loses his temper in violent arguments and is in the thick of many fights throughout. Indeed he may become especially violent when disputing over theology, so the very subject which should have told Adams how wrong he was will be contradicted by his defense of it.

But Fielding does not think any the less of his old friend for all these weaknesses, and we may agree with the mayor in Fielding's *Pasquin,* "A man that won't drink is an enemy to the trade of the nation." Adams is comic partly because he is not what he thinks he is. The austere, classical ideal obtained from ancient literature and philosophy has nothing to do with the good-natured warmth, generosity, and effervescence of his indulgent character, his romantic, adventurous, quarrelsome, independent, and always absent-minded nature. Bergson's now classical theory of the comic man as one who somehow cannot adjust himself to immediate reality, who goes ahead without thinking of the ways of life as it must be continuously lived—such a man is none but Adams in one of his infinite incarnations. His forgetting this or that detail is of course the standard meaning of the term "absent-mindedness" as applied to persons who lead intellectual or abstract lives. But the term describes Adams throughout his entire character. His ludicrous appearance, his clumsiness, his naive inability to do business, his inevitably ending up penniless in negotiating with the publisher even if the sermons had been of any value in money, his blindness to anything that could possibly be of any material advantage to himself, his total incapacity to see through other people—in fact, his own sincerity in such a world as this, Fielding seems to tell us, must remain a sure sign of his unconquerable absent-mindedness. One reason the sermons are worthless is that they are so naively sincere, and perhaps the most touching of all the rare traits in this lovely person, the surest sign of his ignorance, is that he is an honest, convinced, practicing Christian in a world which leaves for a future dispensation the reward of genuine virtue.

The honesty of Adams' religion returns us to the final scene in church. Who does not long to cheer when Adams publicly scolds the pretentious Boobys for their unseemly levity? Here in the house of that religion which he loves so well Adams is vindicated and achieves a dignity that shames the outside, real world, of which he knows nothing. Here at last he seems to be right, and the world a thousand times wrong, and all of his absent-minded incapacity is offset by a dignity that vastly overbalances what his whole life has made to seem irrelevant. No wonder Fielding loved him so well: when showering a benign favor at the story's end, he insures Adams a much-increased income for life, but even in doing so underlines the unchangeable genuineness of Adams by naming the sum of only one-hundred-thirty pounds.

Still, in later years Fielding could not forget Adams and mentions him off and on with approval. Toward the end of *Tom Jones* Fielding cannot leave him out when bestowing every blessing that his worshiped Sophia and the world of Mr. Allworthy could desire. Again we cheer when told that the tyrannical

Thwackum has been banished, that Mr. Allworthy has instead taken Mr. Abraham Adams into his house, that Sophia is very fond of him as every good person must be, and that Adams is to have the tutoring of her children.

Against logic, against even common sense, we rejoice to find our own affection for the man shared by his creator and, in this now best of all imperfect worlds, we salute his coming in and his going out with a glad heart.

Slipslop, Lady Booby, and the Ladder of Dependence

Adams is surely a triumph and might well stand as achievement enough in the comic vein, not to speak of his inexhaustible delight as a character, but he is innocent, and his role for Fielding is rather as a contrast to that vanity and hypocrisy which is essentially ridiculous. Ideas of virtue are shown to be absurd, being propounded for the wrong reasons. Much more ludicrous are the ideas of superiority, people's reasons for thinking that one man is better than another or for imagining that they as individuals should stand above their fellows.

Seeing these notions of high and low, Fielding is almost in despair at human nonsense: "If the Gods, according to the opinion of some, made men only to laugh at them, there is no part of our behaviour which answers the end of our creation better than this." To be sure, it is a very important question who is better, who is in fact higher or lower than others. But men give the wrong answer, an answer which more often than not is irrelevant to the real difference in quality between one person and another. Dividing the human species into the high and the low, we must consider what is meant by these terms.

Now Fielding cannot forbear an ironic thrust, and pretends to offer as figurative what he thinks is real.

He does not mean by "high" any mere physical dimension, "nor metaphorically those of exalted characters or abilities"; this last is precisely what he does mean, that one person is better than another only because of character and ability. But such a notion is so far from exerting any influence in fact that we may as well think of it as a metaphor with many possible applications. Rather one must consider the word "fashion" as the key. Fashion really means dress as called for at any time, and this sense of something merely on the outside is carried throughout Fielding's often indignant comment on human vanity. So a person of fashion looks down upon those of no fashion. They are not fellow Christians, if indeed they are of the same species at all, to be considered as strange persons, creatures, wretches, beasts, brutes, or worst of all as "people one does not know." In general, opinion of relative fashion is based on whether a person has money and ancestry, birth, that is.

But if one is not rich or high-born, any form of social elevation, any accidental advantage of one person over another, so inflates human vanity that even among the lowest gradations there must be a sense of superiority. Let there be one rank between us in the civil order and we consider those lower down "as unworthy to breathe even the same air, and regard the most distant communication with them as an indignity and disgrace offered to ourselves." Fielding often repeats this set of gradations, connections, chains, or ladders as a figure for condemning what is artificial, servile, or ungenuine.

In a *Journey from This World to the Next* preferment is worked out in the frivolous terms of a single smile which is transferred downward from the court favorite, and which in turn takes on the form of a business transaction or promissory note, discounted by the one who first issues it:

> For instance, a very low fellow hath a desire for a place. To whom is he to apply? Not to the great man; for to him he hath no access. He therefore applies to A, who is the creature of B, who is the tool of C, who is the flatterer of D, who is the catamite of E, who is the pimp of F, who is the bully of G, who is the buffoon of I, who is the husband of K, who is the whore of L, who is the bastard of M, who is the instrument of the great man. Thus the smile descending regularly from the great man to A, is discounted back again, and at last paid by the great man.

Every unit in the progression is contemptible, including the husband whose servility and corruption are compounded by being placed alongside so many forms of vicious perversion. So natural distinctions between one man and another are blurred by the demands of an artificial world. Now Fielding studies to offer the most absurd reason imaginable for thinking that one is superior to anyone else; no matter how outlandish or irrelevant it is, it can hardly be worse than what actually obtains in human affairs. In a famous passage in *Joseph Andrews,* he finds that one is better or worse than other men according to the hour of rising every day.

This is as far from having anything to do with true merit as Fielding can think of, yet in fact this distinguishes one man from another in so absurd a world. Dependence is a kind of ladder, a social scale of seven steps: the postilion, the footman, the valet, the squire, the lord, the favorite, and the king. The postilion gets up earliest in the morning and begins brushing the clothes and cleaning the shoes of John the footman. In turn the footman, when he is dressed, waits on Mr. Secondhand the valet who later in the day attends the squire who when equipped goes to the levee of my lord. When this is over, my lord waits upon the levee of the favorite who finally pays homage to the king.

Absurd as the mere existence of such meaningless distinctions must be, Fielding points out that the condescension is greatest, not the higher one is on the ladder, but the lower. In the whole series no one step is "at a greater distance from the other than the first from the second." Letting the snobbery of the high be imitated by the low has the double effect of making them both ridiculous. Triviality in high persons is cheapened when it can be so meaningless as to exist in the same form, or worse, no matter how low one falls in the scheme of things.

Fielding thus exposes servility and meanness by having them emerge among servants even more clearly than among the lords and ladies they are imitating. The essence of affectation is then more obvious in Slipslop and Mrs. Honour than in their betters. Contempt of others is the sign of baseness; the lowest and meanest are most likely to insist on their wretched little margin of superiority, and "the basest mechanic" is generally the most guilty. In a well-known, nicely ambiguous passage in *Tom Jones,* Fielding is puzzled to know why, "but all those who get their living by people of fashion, contract as much insolence to the rest of mankind as if they really belonged to that rank themselves." Their nonsense extends to being proud of the wrong things in their masters. Men servants especially hate to be thought of as serving a pauper; title and fortune in a master make the footman think better of himself, but the reverse is true of virtue and understanding which do not seem to convey respect to anyone but their possessors. Since these do not reflect honor on the domestic, so does their absence reflect no dishonor on him; he hates to seem connected with a beggar, but he thinks nothing of attendance on "a rogue or a blockhead."

Now Fielding admits that this is not so true of women, who observe many varieties of distinction and finer grades of superiority. Here the flatterer and the slave expect to get back from those below the marks of respect already paid to those above.

We return to Fielding's ridicule of Pamela, whose employment is made legal by matrimony; yet she remains the ridiculous fraud she has always been. Pamela withholds her consent to the marriage of her brother Joseph and Fanny on social grounds. Poor Joseph does not know any better than to think that Fanny is at least Pamela's equal; the snobbery of servants is relentless and Pamela is never more servile than in her snobbery after Booby raises her upward. "She was my equal," Pamela says, "but I am no longer Pamela Andrews. I am now this gentleman's lady, and, as such, am above her."

We shall find that Slipslop is above Fanny too by reason of her closeness to an exalted mistress of the Booby line. She is even higher than Joseph in the ladder of dependence, and says rightly that "I am not meat for a footman, I hope." In fact Slipslop is very sensitive to her place in society, taking on the airs of her mistress whenever possible. She is placed in that sensitive borderland where it is easy to confound "the lowest of the high, and the highest of the low," and she is not one to retreat before those who fail to see her exact position. Her formal encounter with Miss Graveairs in which Joseph's use of the stage-coach is disputed reveals her quality as an antagonist. After some preliminary fencing, the question of who is the "betters" of the other comes into the open, Miss Graveairs clearly looking down upon Slipslop and saying she is not used "to converse with servants."

Whereupon Slipslop observes that some people keep no servants to converse with, but she lives in a family with so many servants that "she had more under her own command than any paltry little gentlewoman in the kingdom." Miss Graveairs then makes a serious mistake. The dispute returning to who is the "betters" of whom, each side claiming victory, Miss Graveairs finally threatens to expose the chambermaid's sauciness and will "acquaint your mistress." Slipslop responds with scornful laughter, secure in her position of nearness to one so high that for the moment the borderline between the low high of Miss Graveairs and the high low of Slipslop is obscured, the servant scoring a contemptuous victory with these lofty words: "Her lady was one of the great gentry; and such little paltry gentlewomen, as some folks, who travelled in stage-coaches, would not easily come at her." So a mere access to greatness is enough for contempt of others, and underlines Fielding's derision of its absurdity.

We are led straight to the portals of Lady Booby, past the formidable presence of Slipslop. Upon these Fielding concentrates his genius for irony. We should notice how much Fielding has to say of women in general in the work before us. He contemplates women in areas of behavior wherein they seem more absurd than men; their special forms of nonsense make his case against affectation peculiarly laughable and effective. Fielding has made it clear that he is extremely sympathetic with women, that he does not think them of inferior intelligence; on the contrary, he is inclined to praise and indulge them. He sees that even the finest of women practice a certain amount of deceit so as to make sure of their aims.

From these on down we get many varieties of affected modesty, virtuous bashfulness if it will serve any purpose, concealment, and pretense—all of which deceives only men since women see through each other readily. But Fielding will excuse a good deal of this, especially where love is concerned which "exercises most of the talents of the female or fair world."

He allows himself a kind of pretended amusement or patronization, and says "thou wilt not be angry with the beautiful creatures" considering the way they are brought up to suppress natural affection. One reason for not being angry is in the word "beautiful"; they are the "beautiful part of the creation," he says elsewhere, and seems to enjoy coupling the terms "beautiful" and "creation" when referring to women. While he uses "creature" in other ways, often conventional, Fielding here seems to think of something diminutive, some object to be used, something to be admired and enjoyed for its fine workmanship. He seldom applies the term "creature" to a man, but refers repeatedly in *Joseph Andrews* to "the beauty of this young creature," "the beautiful creatures," and "this lovely creature."

The creatures may be lovely playthings or works of art to be admired, but when they grow up they seem to develop other qualities. Fielding makes his women intensely realistic, deriving amusement from the cynical realism of Slipslop, Lady Booby, Mrs. Tow-wouse, and especially the aunt in his interpolated story of Leonora. A delightful incongruity arises between the supposed delicacy, tenderness, and unselfish romance of women and their actual materialism, predatory determination, and unemotional prudence. Leonora's aunt seems an intentional parallel to the main story. She overcomes the timid scruples of her niece in preferring the advances of the glamorous Bellarmine to her engagement with the prosaic Horatio.

The world, it turns out, is always on the side of prudence and self-interest; money is all that matters and anyone who marries for any other reason will repent. Then one must consider the role of learning in the world as it is: "Besides, if we examine the two men, can you prefer a sneaking fellow, who hath been bred at the university, to a fine gentleman just come from his travels?" When a shift in strategy is called for on the supposed death of Bellarmine in a duel with Horatio, the aunt is grimly determined on victory.

Fielding delights us here with suggestions of military realism and business foresight amid so much romantic emotionalism from Leonora. The aunt adjusts herself quickly to necessary changes in the plan, advises prudence once more, and shows that if one lover is killed by the other Leonora should pursue the live one and not disfigure herself with too much affliction lest this cut off possible offers in the future.

This absence of illusion is carried elsewhere into the eternal rivalry among women who all desire the same thing and must look upon each other as possible obstacles to fulfillment of the common hope. Male admiration for any one becomes a triumph over the others, and each has to preserve the outward marks most likely to inspire an homage that all seek for themselves. Woe betide her who has just left the company or who seems to have a natural advantage in beauty beyond that of her rivals.

Let us admit that Miss Graveairs had behaved badly in the coach, but the onslaught when she has gone is bloody as the others move in for the kill. One after another the women point out her lowness, her lack of gentility, her probable weakness in morals although she is a censorious prude, and worst of all in the opinion of Slipslop, her lack of "compulsion" for poor Joseph which shows that she is no Christian at all but an obvious "Myhummetman." We will, however, find this a pale exercise in annihilation compared with what Slipslop can do to Fanny, the detestable beauty. Her tongue warms up on Pamela when Lady Booby prods her into an opinion of "the dowdy, my niece, I think I am to call her?" This hint was enough, so Slipslop went to work on Pamela "and so miserably defaced her, that it would have been impossible for any one to have known the person." And this, directly after Pamela and Lady Booby had themselves been upset by Mr. Booby's praise of Fanny for which they offered mutual consolation on the ground that men were poor judges of beauty, and while each held up her own looking glass they both contemplated only their own faces and paid "a cross compliment to each other's charms."

To the pedestrian male this might seem a little bordering on meanness and hypocrisy, but the comic spirit sees a vein of realism in women, a tendency to self-justification, a knowledge of one another that comes from the unity of their sex, a general understanding that all women proceed from certain predatory assumptions which are perfectly clear and which make each individual liable to attack and exposure by others.

Fielding makes his commentary on women in *Joseph Andrews* shrewdly comic, especially when he presents Slipslop and her mistress to illustrate vanity and hypocrisy by example, as Adams has done by contrast. Now as we approach the august façade of Slipslop herself a military figure comes irresistibly to mind. Slipslop appears at the head of marvelous phalanxes of embattled females, drawn up in eternal array, all bosomy and baritonal, marching forward in determined pursuit of the common prize. Yet to this prize the entire force of everlasting nature desires only to surrender at discretion, the discretion, however, of those at once attacking and surrendering. Here is one army bent on winning in order to lose, unlike the medieval fight against sin, and Fielding shows that nature itself is on their side.

With Slipslop too, there is something headlong and impetuous in the assault, as of one with no time to spare. Now happily past the change of life any success she might attain could have no third consequence; she could now repay herself for long years of meritorious abstinence. Alas, however, nature had not provided her with a person which would invite that masculine aggression she longed to become the victim of. At forty-five she was short and fat, red, pimply, and bearded of face, with tiny eyes and a bulbous nose set above a protruding, cowlike bosom, the whole unsavory mass carried about on legs of unequal length. She would recall forcibly an old comic friend, the Wife of Bath herself, had it not been for her ill success in their common endeavor.

Slipslop's trouble is at once too nice a delicacy and too high an aspiration. She is unwilling to settle for the company of "stinking old fellows," but longs for the embraces of Joseph himself, young, fresh, and irresistibly handsome. Having prepared him by gentle treatment and various favors, Slipslop approaches the main question with general references to affection and a woman's helpless vulnerability before the advances of a "boy." Joseph—young, simple, and ignorant—is unable to say anything sensible, addressing Slipslop at first as "Madam," and then offering the intolerable insult of love like that for his own mother! This obtuseness infuriates Slipslop, who has not expected that her "passion should be resulted and treated with ironing" or that Joseph will "refer" the society of girls to that of a sensible woman. Slipslop is bent none the less upon this incestuous connection. There follows a delightful parody of epic simile, adding the comedy of heroic elevation to that of sex. Slipslop is now described "as when a hungry tigress" is about to leap on a timid lamb, or a huge and voracious pike prepares to gobble up a tiny fish—the figures from hunting and fishing again emphasizing the predatory attempt with power on one side and utter helplessness on the other. Joseph is delivered by the ringing of a bell summoning Slipslop to her mistress, and the aggressor falls back upon a philosophic realism, accepting her defeat with the aid of a certain "stone-bottle."

If Slipslop appears blind to the deficiencies of her person, she is no less vain of her intellectual pretensions. Fielding makes her "a mighty affecter of hard words"; her pretense takes the form of using words which she cannot pronounce and whose meaning she confuses with others; Joseph mollifies her at one point in their unfortunate interview by expressing respect for her learning. In her disputes with Parson Adams she is able to hold her own by using words in such a way that he is confounded "and would have been much less puzzled by an Arabian manuscript." Slipslop discloses talents, furthermore, as a theological dialectician in combat with Adams; here Fielding compounds the whole absurdity by giving an outlandish reason for Slipslop's intellectual airs: she insists on deference to her understanding, "as she had been frequently at London, and knew more of the world than a country parson could pretend to."

Having been to London is only one of Slipslop's many supports to her vanity. None can seem farther afield than her outcry in the night that rape is about to be committed upon her. This term is connected in *Joseph Andrews* with both Fanny and Slipslop, the one most likely and the other least likely to be obliged to fear it. Fielding seems much amused by talk of rape in view of his implications that male advances are strongly invited, even provoked; certainly, in Slipslop's case, whatever rape is contemplated is by her upon the innocent Joseph, and with respect to her own person it must be considered a pious hope rather than a threatening danger. Fielding is much amused by this pretense, and says in *Tom Jones* that the outcries of imperilled modesty are made largely for their sound. After reluctantly confessing that Jones and Mrs. Waters have been in the same bed, he tells of her awakening when two men fight in the chamber. She screams out "murder" and "robbery" and especially "rape," but Fielding reassures us: "These words of exclamation are used by ladies in a fright . . . only as the vehicles of sound, and without any fixed ideas!"

Now, at the appropriate moment, Slipslop cries out "rape" also and, her lung power being formidable, we can enjoy Fielding's double joke; the louder the outcry the less actual virtue there is, and certainly the less of a threat to what little there may be. It all comes about through the mistake of Beau Didapper who finds himself in bed with Slipslop instead of Fanny after whom he is lusting. He tries to get away, but the vigilant Slipslop sees a chance to give a totally false impression of her chastity. With ludicrous self-deception she tries to make Lady Booby think better of her virtue than she has had reason to do, but again such an idea has to be maintained by force, just as any attack on Slipslop's chastity would have to be imposed on the male aggressor by force.

Here again is Fielding's slyest irony, as Slipslop suddenly catches hold of the retreating Beau, holds him fast in spite of his struggles which she then pretends are her own, roars out against the villain attacking her chastity, ruining her in her sleep when, true enough, it was more likely to happen than during her waking hours. Her outcry of "Murder! murder! rape! robbery! ruin!" is a histrionic triumph, its absurd artificiality being suggested by alliteration of the letter "r." The noise brings poor Adams on the run, and it is some time before in the confusion and darkness he discovers "by the two mountains which Slipslop carried before her, that he was concerned with a female." Lady Booby enters, Slipslop again gets credit for a cry for help, her mistress in turn pretends modest shock at sight of Adams' undressed state, and he, the innocent Don Quixote unselfishly rushing to the aid of threatened goodness, is the object of torrential abuse for his bestiality.

It seems that Fielding is not taken in by Slipslop's pretense either to learning or to virtue. Her third main affectation, of social superiority, is equally remote. She overcomes Miss Graveairs to be sure, and we recall that among her points of pride is this, that she has more servants under her command than some persons of the minor gentry themselves. Among these is the illiterate Fanny, whose beauty is an unforgivable offense. Even Mrs. Adams rails at her as a "vagabond slut" and Slipslop herself offers the most disdainful snub in pretending not to remember even who she is. Fanny curtsies to the great presence and offers to come up to her; "but that high woman" will not return the compliment. Casting her eyes elsewhere she withdraws, wondering audibly "who the creature was." She conceals her frustration at not getting Joseph herself by refusing "to admit any such trollops" as Fanny, while poor Adams in his ignorant simplicity has run after her to say that Fanny is one of her old acquaintances whom she has apparently forgotten—"Do but see what a fine woman she is grown since she left Lady Booby's service." Slipslop allows that perhaps she does "reflect" something of her, but of course "I can't remember all the inferior servants in our family." And toward the end, when Fanny's triumph is not far off, Slipslop joins her mistress in an exercise of primitive female surgery upon a more attractive rival. Here Fielding subtly draws together the three main lines of Slipslop's affectation as to sex, learning, and social superiority. He lets her fall upon Fanny "whom she hacked and hewed in the like barbarous manner, concluding . . . that there was always something in those low-life creatures which must eternally extinguish them from their betters."

It is often remarked that Lady Booby and Slipslop derive from the same comic materials. Each is a great deal clearer for the similarity than she would be alone. But the one who stands higher in the social scale becomes more laughable in Fielding's eyes. Neither of these affected ladies in any case can escape the truth of her own nature, and social standing becomes the more irrelevant when they appear so much alike. Both are lecherous, affected, snobbish, authoritarian, and unreasonable, full of contradiction and absurd self-deception. Fielding lets their near equality as human beings come through from the outset as they both try to seduce Joseph, and are both quite rightly unsuccessful.

After her own marked failure, Slipslop applies an omnivorous ear to the keyhole while her mistress is in turn being repulsed by Joseph; we are back in recollection with the fat abbot eavesdropping outside the closed cell, another broad bottom and red face before us, a façade of bloated self-indulgence contradicting pretenses to the opposite.

Now Slipslop shows how easy it would be for her to rise from her servile condition when she has the impudence to act as if her knowing the secret she has just overheard places her on an equality with Lady Booby. She is now pleased to object to her lady's capricious orders. She catches up the main word or expression in each sentence of her mistress, has the face to question it with an exasperating arrogance. But having gone so far toward showing that she and her mistress are more or less the same, Slipslop with that realistic prudence we have so often admired decides to keep a position that is after all a fact to be depended on. At the right moment she adopts a suitable condescension, and the two precious sisters are reconciled.

Our lines converge at last upon Lady Booby, a woman of fashion, of quality, of figure, of condition, of distinction, of condescension. She is really, as Fielding says, the heroine of the story, in that she is the essence of what the novel has set out to ridicule. Lady Booby thinks herself vastly above other people, socially and morally better than they are. She ends in defeat on both counts through loving Joseph, a mere footman, and in being rejected by him because he is morally concerned to keep a virtue that on her own side she wishes to surrender.

Fielding does not develop much sympathy for Lady Booby, save now and then in moments when she is genuinely tormented by feelings that she cannot help. But there are some things that the most tolerant of comic artists cannot approve, and one of these is the unjustified arrogance of his heroine. He even lets her show a form of personal cruelty which he clearly despised, when Lady Booby invites her company for a walk and promises them a diversion, "one of the most ridiculous sights they had ever seen, which was an old foolish parson, who, she said laughing, kept a wife and six brats on a salary of about twenty pounds a year," the most ragged family in the parish. Her humor is twice indefensible, as being malicious and as being directed at Adams, the symbol of a goodness to which she can never pretend.

But people of quality live as they please and set up any standard they like. How low and artificial this can be is suggested by Lady Booby's compromise with such a piece of trash as Slipslop in the first place, and by her reasons for it in the next. Everything turned on her reputation, and she would not have desired to fall so low as Lady Bellaston in *Tom Jones,* "whom everybody knows to be what nobody calls her." Lady Booby must not be known for what she was, nor must she be called it; hence the need to be reconciled with Slipslop who if dismissed might have spoiled her reputation. On this depended so many of the blessings in her life—"particularly cards, making curtsies in public places and, above all, the pleasure of demolishing the reputation of others, in which innocent amusement she had an extraordinary delight." If no one suspected the truth, Lady Booby could go on wasting her life in triviality and satisfying the meanness of her spirit in hypocritical malice.

But her pretentious assumption of superiority gains nothing; defeat stares her in the face, and she must see the desired prize of Joseph's person fall to the beauteous but low-born Fanny. The girl's loveliness would have infuriated her at any social level; one woman can hardly applaud the special advantages of another as all go forward in the common enterprise.

But Fanny's beauty is a fact of nature, and it is nature with which Lady Booby's assumptions must finally collide. She tries to prevent the marriage of Fanny and Joseph, which she hates on personal grounds, by using the influence of her august position. Her furious commentary both to Adams against the banns and to Lawyer Scout against the law constantly repeats two words: the pronoun "I" and the abstract term "beauty"; so Fielding brings out after his fashion her twofold bitterness and arrogance, the fury of a woman scorned to begin with, but a woman superior to the object of her desire and so adding a social defeat from nature to a personal one. Adams of course in his innocent, elephantine pursuit of what is right and good favors the marriage and foolishly describes Fanny as the handsomest woman ever to come into the parish. He is overwhelmed by a torrent of outraged egotism: Adams is impertinent to speak so to such an eminence. To apply the term beauty to a country wench is absurd, as if all good things and even the very terms for what life most admired had necessarily to apply upward in society first.

Fanny is not to be allowed "to stock the parish with beauties" and to multiply the already too numerous poor; again the terms reveal new dimensions of arrogance and unfeeling disdain, the terms of animal breeding on one hand and social nuisance on the other. Lady Booby must in the end condemn herself for the humility and condescension of her discourse with Adams, and ends her lofty statement in four sentences every one of which is dominated by "I" and what "I" will permit or decree. "I tell you," "I repeat," "I desire," "I will have" is all she can offer in defeat. She can do little better in trying to circumvent the law when she is informed that a year's service gains a settlement in the parish, so that no sentence of banishment will be effective even though Fanny and Joseph should proliferate monstrously and settle a pack of wretched beggars and vagabonds, however beautiful, on the parish. Her egotism is here surpassed only by her failure in logic as she bluntly announces, "I am resolved . . . to have no discarded servants of mine settled here; and so, if this be your law, I shall send to another lawyer."

But time begins to run out, and Lady Booby must come at her dilemma more effectively. She will accept Joseph, she tells her brother; but she cannot admit Fanny, who is unnamed in this sentence, but included among "all the dirty trollops in the country." Lusting after Joseph, she has yet the hypocrisy to invoke her social condescension in allowing him to sit at her table. So her desire, a fact of nature like Joseph's charm, conflicts with her social arrogance which is so precious to her that to the end she tries to get Joseph for herself while remaining within acceptable snobbish terms.

Now Joseph's brother-in-law is to do all possible to dissuade him from the match with Fanny; then Joseph may be placed in some genteel post, perhaps in the army with a commission. From such a gentleman's plane, Joseph's "accomplishments might quickly gain him an alliance which would not be to their discredit." So when nature conflicts with custom, Lady Booby seeks to appease both sides.

Her fury can only grow—she is furious socially and emotionally and, because Fielding never lets her natural passion really overcome her social arrogance, he makes sure that we do not sympathize too strongly with his heroine, his prime instance of ridiculous affectation. When she wants Joseph most violently for herself, Lady Booby can still curse him for his lowness, "which can basely descend to this despicable wench, and be ungratefully deaf to all the honours I do him." Now she wouldn't have him anyway, she says, but she will see to it that no one else gets him instead; to her final defeat she is allowed to suffer doubly, because as a human being she is so lost in the wrongness of her social vanity that she cannot experience a natural feeling without it.

If vanity and snobbery so control Lady Booby's life and character, perhaps it will seem proper that we have carried her to the last encounter first and have saved to the end her pretenses of virtue and honor, her temptation of Joseph and his rejection of her in one of the most famous of comic scenes.

Lady Booby's vain and arrogant assumptions were no doubt common enough in her day; that she was better and higher than other people she would consider axiomatic as would most others of her class. But nature did not seem always to agree with this, and the facts did not sustain her artificial view of life. If one fell in love, there might be a difference between what really was, and what one assumed, and at this point Lady Booby began her own collision with reality. Fielding might well make his point even if Lady Booby had been enamored of someone much higher on the ladder of dependence than Joseph; he underlines it past confusion by fixing Joseph almost at the bottom, where he was none the less observed by his mistress and became the object of her passion. She did everything possible to encourage Joseph's response, indulging him in "all those innocent freedoms which women of figure may permit without the least sully of their virtue."

Unlike Bridget Allworthy, who in later life was on vigilant guard against the snares laid for female honor, Lady Booby seems to have set traps of her own so as to make certain of a loss which she none the less must pretend to fear. Fielding likes to maintain that caution is greatest in women whose danger is least, and that virtue is courted most by those who have no real chance to lose it. Lady Booby in any case was doing all she could to increase what danger there was, great or small.

Meanwhile the obtuse Joseph gave no sign that he understood what was expected of him, and it is hard to say what might have gone forward if a most unhappy accident had not intervened. Lady Booby suffered the inexpressible loss of her husband Sir Thomas Booby, who died suddenly, leaving his disconsolate widow in sorrowing loneliness. Her love for him was one of those nobly sustained emotions, carried within her for years, and prevented from its naturally tempestuous expression by that delicacy and reticence for which Lady Booby was distinguished.

Later on, when reminiscing over her marriage in the presence of Slipslop, the widow confides that her husband never obtained so much as a kiss from her "without my expressing reluctance in the granting it. I am sure he himself never suspected how much I loved him." Here the ironic double meaning is rich indeed. We know that Sir Thomas has not been dead a week before his spouse is eagerly trying to bestow on Joseph what she has with such delicacy restrained throughout her married life. Joseph is called to bring up her teakettle and finds his lady in bed. By accident, she lays her hand on his which leads to her question "if he had ever been in love." Joseph's reserve continues, yet Lady Booby even at this crisis in her plans cannot omit reference to the social difference between them and wonders whether her reputation might be safe in case she were to admit Joseph to certain familiarities which he might expect from an equal. Assured of his discretion, Lady Booby has occasion to raise herself in bed, disclosing "one of the whitest necks that ever was seen," so that Joseph blushes.

This leads to the word "honour," a mere word indeed, referring here to something she longs to be rid of. In affected surprise, the lady cries, "What am I doing? I have trusted myself with a man alone, naked in bed; suppose you should have any wicked intentions upon my honour, how should I defend myself?" Lady Booby refers to the word and nothing else; she invites its violation by mentioning it, since if it is genuine she needs only to observe it as part of herself. To speak of it at all is to provoke aggression against it and to show that it has no real existence. To mention it is a signal to Joseph to proceed with his attack, eliminating Lady Booby's honor as an obstacle to any impulses he might have.

All this seems lost on Joseph; as he says, he fails to

understand the increasing ambiguity of his lady's discourse. She begins to lose her temper at what is surely his pretended innocence and, when he protests his fidelity to her and his late master, she falls back on grief for the departed and dismisses Joseph for having tormented her by mention of her dead husband.

At this point it is only fair to offer Lady Booby our sympathy. Since she is of higher rank than he, she must make the first signs, like a queen asking the future consort to marry her. Lady Booby must then hint to Joseph that his advances would be welcome, and we must excuse a few preliminary moves from her as befits the difference in their stations. But once this is done she expects a fuller response, indeed a more than common fervor in view of the release her condescension has given to something which must be held back until her consent is obtained. The main problem then is her consent not, surely, whether a man lower in society than herself would conceivably hesitate to proceed if she allows it. As for his virtue's being a factor, it never occurs to her until he mentions it, and then a full two minutes must elapse before she can even utter a sound.

Now after Joseph's departure a dialogue ensues between the precious Slipslop and her mistress, wherein certain grave charges are levelled against the unhappy footman. The lady piously resolves to free the household of such a dangerous young rake, but love is again troublesome and only after four different changes of mind does she send for Joseph with the aim of first insulting and then discharging him from her service.

Here Fielding artfully inserts a description of Joseph's magnificent physical attractions, thus establishing the reason that all of Lady Booby's pretenses are merely that and nothing more. Fielding wishes us to admit a very great temptation indeed, and we cannot condemn women for falling when the temptation is so great. This means that we may never condemn them at all, since they have no interest in falling unless there is great temptation. He seems to imply that all this is not concerned with real evil, with vice or virtue as such; we have an impulse of human nature with no harm in it, save that imposed by conventions and codes, which he is out to ridicule.

Now Lady Booby looking at this toothsome fellow begins to scold Joseph for his behavior to the servant girls as charged by Slipslop. These accusations astonish him, but he is only being accused of what one would expect him to be guilty of. If he is not, there must be something the matter with him. Certainly Lady Booby assumes that the charges are true, and indeed is much encouraged by them; for if they are true then Joseph might well be tempted, as she tells him to "do better," as it can hardly be that he has any moral scruples. Why not then have him for herself, since he is so promiscuous?

But he continues to assert his innocence, maintaining that he has never gone beyond kissing. The use of such an intimate term brings a sudden blush to the cheek of his reserved mistress, who first announces that a kiss is only the prolog to greater liberties; any woman who grants a kiss will surely grant more, and so on. Now, however, comes the question that Joseph is obliged to answer: "If I should admit you to such freedom, what would you think of me?—tell me freely."

At this point it is Joseph who introduces the note of social distinction when his lady has at last brought herself to put it aside: "I should think your ladyship condescended a great deal below yourself." What might a short while before have been a prime motive with Lady Booby is now brushed aside in the excitement and impatience of accelerated hope! "Pugh!" said she, "That I am to answer to myself." What really matters now is whether Joseph would be contented with only a kiss, whether indeed this would not inflame his inclinations to demand more.

If the comic finds its essence in the unexpected, the famous answer of Joseph at this critical moment becomes a stroke of genius. Referring then to the inclinations which Lady Booby assumes to set on fire, Joseph solemnly replies, "Madam . . . if they were, I hope I should be able to control them, without suffering them to get the better of my virtue."

Fielding wishes to be certain that we do not miss the power and greatness of this moment. He offers a preposterous mixture of figures from ancient literature, history, and art along with references to contemporary drama, ending with a tribute to the "inimitable pencil of my friend Hogarth," all intended to suggest the surprise that overcomes Lady Booby at Joseph's words.

Two minutes pass before she is able to utter a sound, so dumbfounded is she at the very notion that virtue, as embodied in chastity, is more than a word. Since women are supposed to have virtue in this sense and men are not, and since in fact women are only interested in finding, as a rule, a man attractive enough to lose it to, the whole affair is a mere concept. Lady Booby has been under the impression that virtue was a female trait which meant that it belonged only to women's usual façade. Now she must make some answer to Joseph after his unthinkably obtuse failure to understand the plain facts. Fielding again skillfully shows us the two sides of

Lady Booby that are uppermost—sex and snobbery, desire and personal vanity.

> "Your virtue!" said the lady, recovering after a silence of two minutes. "I shall never survive it. Your virtue!—intolerable confidence! Have you the assurance to pretend, that when a lady demeans herself to throw aside the rules of decency, in order to honour you with the highest favour in her power, your virtue should resist her inclination? that when she had conquered her own virtue, she should find an obstruction in yours?"

Joseph still persists in referring to his virtue as a reality which should be taken into account, whereas Lady Booby is entirely out of patience. No human being has ever heard of a man's virtue before, and it is incredible that a mere boy should "have the confidence to talk of his virtue." It is all doubly a negation, because what is discussed is never real even for the women who profess it, not to mention for men who are supposed to play a kind of game, observing the rules as laid down by a commonly understood and tacitly accepted, but never actually stated, pretense.

Joseph's apology is too late; he has not wished to offend his lady, but he has done so past recall. Amid frustrated efforts to cover up her now obvious intent, and her furious sense of outrage and defeat, Lady Booby dismisses Joseph from the room. At long last she brings herself to discharge him from her service, so that he sets out on the journey that absorbs the center of Fielding's novel.

Joseph's ill-fortune, to be sure, could have been predicted from any manual of behavior for those who wish to stand well in the world. The Abbé Bellegarde has said that people who are above us in quality or birth "can't bear we should excel, or even equal them, in the qualities which they value themselves upon." This is true of virtue as well as other talents, especially if the virtue is more pretended than real. Again it is not only a violation of the laws of war between the sexes for Joseph to stand on his virtue after Lady Booby has offered to surrender hers: it is simply bad manners and foolish ill-breeding for a low-life servant to seem to possess qualities higher than his superior can show. So poor Joseph is out of order from this side of Lady Booby's two main convictions as well.

What shall we say then of Fielding's heroine, but to remark finally on what a triumph of his ironic genius she is? He uses the one natural and human thing in her to punish the affectation she can never conquer. Adams' vanity does no harm, but Lady Booby's weakness is different. She is punished when a fact of nature, her falling in love with Joseph, conflicts with her absurd assumption that she is better than other people. She is defeated by reality too, just as Adams is buffeted by life as it is. Lady Booby's affectation is just as far from conforming to nature and justice and right, which are an ultimate if not a present reality, as Adams' own quixotic devotion to learning and ideal Christianity are from coinciding with immediate reality. And although love is her punishment Lady Booby does not retreat from her false position. Her defeat does not chasten or improve her, so she gets little of our sympathy; say what we will of Slipslop, she at least would love a footman and marry him if it suited her. But in nature the footman may love someone else, an illiterate housemaid; so love has the last word and prevails over snobbery.

If love and pity had won out in Lady Booby over honor, pride, and revenge our feelings would be different toward her. Although she pretends to hate the "tyranny of custom," she will be governed by it in the end. She cannot escape the notion that if she were to forget social demands and marry Joseph anyway, it would be a favor, a condescension on her part. So long as she is of this opinion, Fielding will never permit her to marry anyone whom he loves. He has her condescend to what she had no chance to obtain anyway, and so exposes the nothingness of her assumed superiority.

Perhaps what Jonathan Wild says of himself is true of all vain characters: "I had rather stand on the summit of a dunghill, than at the bottom of a hill in Paradise." Those who will be high, who will affect an elevation above others, who will try to seem what they are not in nature and will pretend to what other men must confess themselves too weak to achieve—all such will incur the enmity of Henry Fielding and must expect to hear the derision of his laughter.

Mr. Micawber's Difficulties

Pausing now amid these illustrations of discerning tolerance, the reader, with Boccaccio's abbot in mind, will have seen a greater complexity in Fielding's response. Fielding shares the amusement and generosity of a great medieval humanist, but is bent on conveying moral lessons which call as much upon his indignation and severity of judgment as compassion. Yet his view is clear at all times, with little of the ambiguity surrounding that superb creation of Dickens, Wilkins Micawber. Comic treatment of failure that is hard to distinguish from wickedness raises the question of how Dickens manages to leave us with affection for someone whose surface behavior is intolerable. Micawber may be, as J. B. Priestley says, the greatest comic creation in English except Falstaff, but he remains a baffling figure whose secret may in the end elude us.

Chesterton, who is still indispensable on Dickens, is content to be grateful. He finds available criticism of little help; the critics "have only walked 'round and 'round Micawber wondering what they should say. I am myself walking 'round and 'round Micawber wondering what I shall say. And I have not found out yet."

More recently Mr. A. O. J. Cockshut in the *Imagination of Charles Dickens* has remarked that "Everybody can appreciate Mr. Micawber, but what can the critic say about him? . . . To read of Mr. Micawber is . . . a deeply felt experience, but it is not susceptible of analytic description."

Now let us go over his part once again, enjoying Micawber for what he is, hoping to draw closer to him through a fresh reading. We will put Mrs. Micawber to one side with a promise of early return. Meanwhile, to attempt a solution for Mr. Micawber's complexity, we must pay close attention to his power as a literary and theatrical artist. Keeping in mind that Micawber is a man of letters and an actor, reaching his fulfillment in writing and speaking, we behold in turn the superman himself, his appearance and overall impression, his essential happiness in spite of all difficulties, his peculiar mode of expression, his moral character, and Dickens' final resolution of his fate.

Wilkins Micawber presents himself to Mr. Quinion at Murdstone and Grinby's where little David Copperfield sees him for the first time. His appearance as then described never changes, except briefly when he is reduced to a disguise, and when he is involved in the refinements of Wickfield, Heep, and Co. David sees a man of uncertain middle age, rather stout in figure, totally bald on his large and shiny head, wearing a brown surtout, black tights and shoes, and a high "imposing shirt-collar." In addition he carries a cane with a large pair of rusty tassels, and a kind of monocle which hangs outside his coat, purely for ornament. The general effect is rather shabby yet distinguished in a certain way.

Micawber speaks with an air of condescension, gentility, and confidence, so that from the very outset he establishes the contradictions of his nature. Micawber always tries to seem what he is not and cannot ever be: important, youthful, genteel, upperclass, learned, and fashionable; but he turns out to be all façade, manner, rhetoric, trappings, suits, and airs. His very occupation when we first see him is nothing tangible carried on by himself. He is supposed to travel and sell things on commission, sometimes grain, sometimes anything else which he cannot sell, so as to leave himself penniless. The summary of his work at this point carries just the right suggestions of vagueness, generality, and diffused futility: "He was a sort of town traveller for a number of miscellaneous houses now, but made little or nothing of it I am afraid."

It is agreed that Micawber will show David the way that evening to the house in Windsor Terrace where a room has been taken for him. In a touching passage poor little David speaks of Mr. Micawber's arrival, of having "washed my hands and face, to do the greater honour to his gentility." But on arrival at the house in Windsor Terrace, we get the same impression of an attempt to be something which does not quite succeed. The place is shabby, too, and like Micawber it makes all the show possible. Since there is no furniture on the first floor, the blinds are kept down to mislead the neighbors.

Then there are Mrs. Micawber, the perpetually nursing twin or twins, two other children under the age of five, plus the dilapidated and snorting Clickett, servant to the family. The proliferation of children only emphasizes that there is nothing to feed or clothe them with, and signifies that they are themselves part of the difference between what really is and what is pretended. If one has children, one should provide for them; having healthy children suggests abundance and well-being. But, like the general airs of their parents, the little Micawbers are only a façade, and really aggravate the common distress. So also with Mrs. Micawber's brass plate on the door and its engraved letters "Mrs. Micawber's Boarding Establishment for Young Ladies." Characteristically a brass plate puts forth this special pretense, not just a cardboard sign that means nothing. Of course, no young lady has ever been there, none has ever proposed to come or would find anything to come to if she did.

In fact, no one ever comes except creditors, those awkward, inconvenient, vulgar symbols of reality. As in *Don Quixote* and *Joseph Andrews,* reality takes the form of having to pay money. And money is hard, necessary, inflexible, unable to be anything other than what it is, and so completely foreign to Micawber's specially invented world.

The creditors would arrive, demanding payment; Mr. Micawber would be in agonies of "grief and mortification"; the "difficulties" and the "embarrassments" so often referred to as temporary would reach one of their crises, because they were not temporary but perpetual, Mr. Micawber might threaten himself with a razor, as this weapon could be made to seem so much more terrifying in its sharpness than any other; after a time the creditors would go away frustrated and the crisis would be over. In half an hour "He would polish up his shoes with extraordinary pains, and go out, humming a tune with a greater air of gentility than ever," the polish itself a new evasion or concealment, helping to show that all was well.

Micawber is only one more, but a triumphant example, of that happiness of the unhappy so often remarked in Dickens. The best time is had by those with the least reason for it. They represent the principle of happiness that Santayana finds in Aristotle: "It is spontaneous life of any sort harmonized with circumstances." Certainly Micawber is able to overcome any disharmony with circumstances, to adjust himself to difficulties, and to discover in the fact that nothing ever has turned up an absolute certainty that something will. Micawber continues to be happy because he is adjustable, highly flexible, and as versatile in the parts he can play as an actor in a repertory theatre.

This view of Micawber as an actor aims at the center of his character. Certainly he is never so much an artist playing a complex role as when pretending that he is a practical businessman. We hear that he was once an officer in the Marines, but when he begins to stride across the pages of *David Copperfield* he is engaged in selling on commission. Since he cannot sell, he gets no commission, and continues to hold the kind of post that commits a given firm to the absolute minimum. But the artist seeming to be what as a person he never could be is successful in the pretense, the acting. So Micawber in his time plays many parts: businessman, entrepreneur, traveling salesman, commission merchant, baker, broker, brewer, landlord, petitioner of His Majesty, member of a learned profession, and in the end colonial adventurer, pioneer, farmer, weather-beaten sailor, journalist, and public servant.

Who would not be happy in a life so various, all mankind's epitome indeed? And Micawber's enjoyment is the greater the more removed from practical benefit his activity is. His pleasure depends on not having any reason to be glad about anything; the less likelihood there is of getting what he expects will turn up, the more grandly does he announce its coming. Assuming that his advertisement in the papers will cause "something satisfactory" to turn up, Micawber decides on new living quarters which he describes minutely with the changes he will have to make in them, at length begging the company "to forgive his having launched into these practical and business-like details, and to excuse it as natural in one who was making entirely new arrangements in life." The more outlandish his expectations, the more "practical" he regards them; his gayety goes on regardless of the facts.

Micawber overcomes difficulties by acting as if they did not exist, or by even seeing a virtue in them. His troubles are necessary to him; he enlarges and hangs on to them as if they let him display a courage that would never show itself without adequate troubles to overcome. He boasts of his tribulations, and even if in despair at the imminence of arrest or a new crisis he will happily order something on credit so as to increase the very troubles he suffers from. His difficulties become a source of pride, showing how valiant was his fight against them. He never lets on that the troubles themselves imply that he is incompetent; problems let Micawber play the role of victim on one hand, and heroic conqueror of life's obstacles on the other. The movement of his life is not a natural one toward success, but a retreat from disaster; Micawber contends against failure, not for success. Without difficulties to overcome, his life is not only empty but alarming. Nothing suggests this dependence on ruin so much as the time spent in debtor's prison.

We find the great man at his summit when he is in jail; he is free only when under arrest. Micawber has the time of his life dining in the security of imprisonment, sending his compliments to Captain Hopkins by David and would he please lend a knife and fork, composing a petition on behalf of "His Gracious Majesty's unfortunate subjects," hearing the document read with a smile as of "an author's vanity," not thinking that if he had anything to be vain about he would not be where he was or writing such a petition.

The day of release finds Micawber utterly miserable; David has never seen him so wretched. Once out of jail, he cannot feel the same hopes or illusions. Jail protects him from life, from the need of working toward the success he can pretend is possible so long as jail prevents him from doing anything about it. Micawber himself refers to his imprisonment later on as the period when he was on "glorious terms" with his fellow man, able to look him in the face or punch his head, secure from the pressure of "pecuniary liabilities," free at long last from creditors, process-servers, and detainers. In fact, were it not for "the impiety of the aspiration," he would wish that he had never passed this landmark in his career.

So vivid is the remembrance of prison days that Micawber ends the last of his letters written in England with a reference to his final arrest and the ending of his days in prison for debt; his very epitaph, to be seen by some passerby in future years, will be an inscription on the prison wall—"With a rusty nail. The obscure initials W.M."

Like Micawber's transcendent happiness in jail is the joy he gets out of activity which cannot profit him. Orwell says that the end of Dickens' finest comic scenes is to show the inherent decency of ordinary human nature. Micawber warms us like Dickens' other amiable creations: he is an excellent friend who, while helpless to do anything for himself, is totally unselfish when acting for others. He may be, as Chesterton says, a confounded nuisance, but "it is better to have a bad debt and a good friend," as even Traddles would say.

Micawber can never be active on his own behalf, so he has to wait for things "to turn up" of themselves.

The petition shows his good nature, as Dickens says, shows that he could be "as active a creature about everything but his own affairs as ever existed, and never so happy as when he was busy about something that could never be of any profit to him." Here his interest contradicted his capacity; everything about him made success impossible. He did not lack talent, as his wife says; he lacked only money; that is, anything which could do him actual good.

His virtues are all general, liberal, and humane. He can be a candidate for any opening, announcing his availability in the newspapers, the vaguest, most transitory, and least substantial of media. He and his wife find Micawber suited to all well-paid positions, able to assume any responsibilities. In fact things are going badly in the world for lack of his services. He envies no one, but is himself superior to a blind world that fails to recognize how much good he could do if given the chance. In his personal life he is an affectionate friend, a devoted husband and father, and as we add up his virtues we see clearly that Micawber possesses every good quality but, alas, one!

We are glad when such a man lives happily, in spite of the agonies endured through "temporary" embarrassments. For along with all of his gayety and confidence Micawber suffers a great deal. Although he rises above his sufferings by creating large figures of speech in which to express them, the fact remains that by so much weeping and fainting he and Mrs. Micawber have often seemed to merit the luxurious quantities of eating and drinking they do at other times. Swooning belongs more to the portrait of Mrs. Micawber but, in contrast to the symbols of enjoyment and gay profusion that are being consumed so much of the time, Micawber himself on at least five occasions is dissolved in tears, "unfeignedly sobbing," being flooded with tears or mingling his tears with others. But we remember the celebrated buoyancy by which he can rise from the pit of gloom into the empyrean of happiness, and on such occasions no man derives a keener enjoyment from the good things of bar and table.

Now everyone knows that there is a great deal of eating and drinking in English literature, especially in the novel, concerned with what actually happens in life every day. Readers of Dickens are fond of drawing up vast, swollen catalogues of what is consumed in the course of one of his early novels; we hear that *Pickwick* for example, is an incessant parade of repasts of all kinds wherein out of fifty-seven chapters forty-three have to do with eating and/or drinking in some form.

Dickens was himself very moderate, but he understood his characters so well and was so devoted to their welfare and enjoyment that he provided for them with a father's indulgence.

This is true even when, as with Dick Swiveller and Micawber, they have no chance to pay for what is consumed. Apart from a number of suppers, breakfasts, and teas of unspecified ingredients, we sit down with the Micawbers at various times to veal cutlet, cheese, loin of mutton, lamb's fry, shrimps, loin of pork, apple sauce, pudding, kidney pie, ale, brandy and water, flip, breaded lamb chops, fish, roast loin of veal, red sausage meat, partridge, wine, leg of mutton and gravy, pigeon pie, and—every time there is the least excuse for it—punch, veritable lakes of punch.

Here was a mighty "power of suction" indeed, as

Tony Weller says, and in the consumption or, better still, the preparation of punch there is a symbol of Micawber's whole portrait: his enjoyment of life while contributing as host to the pleasure of others. Punch is a means of imbibing general consolation, and so Micawber seems to combine in himself the despair of our human condition and the means of relief all at once. Punch itself, preparing it, and serving it to others summarizes what Micawber seems able to do in life. The making of punch out of rum, lemon peel, hot water, and sugar demands just the kind of bustling activity, amid a great apparatus of utensils and materials, that Micawber loves.

A big bowl of miscellaneous materials, abundant and steaming there for everyone to enjoy with gay sociability, ladled out by Micawber as host with fulsome rhetoric and sonorous gayety and business—it is the perfect setting for a life of profitless enjoyment. David's party calls up this side of Micawber's genius, and who does not long to have been present? David never saw anyone so thoroughly enjoy himself as Micawber bending over the ingredients; he looked as if he were creating "instead of punch, a fortune for his family down to the latest posterity."

So Micawber's happiness depends on his playing, among many parts, that of convivial host. It relies in turn upon his command of words, for Micawber's greatness as a man of letters is inseparable from his troubles. He uses words at once to obscure his troubles from himself and others, to make them seem less threatening, and to get relief from them by their expression. When dreadful things happen he hides them under a cloud of figurative terms or makes them blend into glowing images.

We should guard against a charge sometimes heard against Dickens himself, that he will not use one word where ten will do. Dickens can be subtly economical in using words, and even for comic effect invents the elliptical Mr. Jingle of *Pickwick* with his stenographic style. Although he enjoys the verbosity of Micawber, Dickens steps out of the book to tell us of the danger in such excess, and how it may bring the nation into trouble, as in the past when England maintained "too large a retinue of words."

The English are supposed to have solved problems through not calling things by their actual names, so we can be happy that Dickens has made Micawber so English in letting him get out of trouble by expressing it with extravagance. Sam Weller's pronunciation and grammar are grossly improper but they underline his absolute genuineness; so Micawber's abstract terms, learned allusions, quotations, sonorous periods, and complex figures show that he can never be in fact what he seems to be in words.

Again, Micawber's language is allied to the pleasure he gets from his troubles. Like Dick Swiveller he finds the cure and relief of suffering in its expression. He utters his misery so well that he ceases to be miserable in the delight that his literary creation gives him—the catharsis of a satisfying utterance. He is once more the artist for whom his art is an end in itself, able to correct the sorrow that called it forth.

When things become desperate, Micawber's imagination frees him, and he needs only to intensify his rhetoric to cover the new disaster; he can enjoy every new crisis, because it will lay new demands on his powers as an artist to create terms and figures in which to obscure or eliminate it. Thus dreadful facts disappear, or are transformed, and disaster becomes an asset to artistic creation as it is clothed in the purple rhetoric and eloquence of a great artist.

What difference does it make that Micawber is poor when the glories of language can make him rich again? He seems like a man of independent wealth when he finishes telling how desperate his situation is. And which is the greater wealth after all? Is not Micawber right as Don Quixote is right, and the meddling world impertinent? Certainly these heroic figures see nothing absurd in their claims, and Micawber himself glories in what seems ridiculous to the plodding world of money. In his oration exposing the wickedness of Heep, he is enchanted by a Shakespearean figure and grows so fond of it in the reading that he pretends to have lost his place in the manuscript thus obliging him to repeat "that universal applicability which distinguishes the illustrious ornament of the Elizabethan Era." David reports that Micawber "appeared majestically refreshed by the sound" of his own words, and found special delight in a series of abstractions by which he described his career, "a prey to . . . dismal calamities."

This vast pleasure in literary catharsis comes through in all of Micawber's language. His conversation would serve if we had nothing else, but he loves to write letters, a form ideally suited to his genius. Including the last missive from Australia and his oration against Heep, we are enriched by eight letters; these, taken with the great man's fluent conversation, are a monument of solemn absurdity.

We are told that Micawber is supremely funny without ever saying a thing that he himself considers laughable. He simply achieves a preposterous effect by what he says and writes. The discourse of this ridiculous failure absorbs material from great authors and masterpieces, which he rephrases in a heavily Latinized, abstract vocabulary with a marked 18th-century, neoclassical flavor, plus an endless profusion of metaphors describing his troubles. Micawber uses what we would expect of a wise man wishing to convey the lessons of experience: the Bible, classical mythology, and proverbial utterances of various kinds. In addition he relies heavily on Shakespeare, Chaucer, and a number of 18th-century figures like Grey, Johnson, Pope, Edward Young, and Burns.

Besides direct reliances on neoclassical authors, Micawber often uses the balance and antithesis of his models to sustain his own pomp. Accidents, it seems, "may be expected with confidence and must be borne with philosophy."

Whatever station in society he may attain through the legal profession, "I shall endeavour not to disgrace, and Mrs. Micawber will be safe to adorn." He is fond of the formal address "Sir" as befits an 18th-century gentleman, and invokes the Horatian principle of delight and instruction as the aim of literature.

The skillful use of anticlimax is one of the delights of Augustan poetry, but Micawber's celebrated examples of it hardly recall *The Rape of the Lock.* For him, anticlimax comes of the habit of inflating everything, blowing it up with false eloquence and then floundering to the ground with "in short." Micawber is so involved and tangled in his own rhetoric that he must stop and turn around when he can no longer go on. Once more he underlines his inability to be what he tries to be. He cannot quite bring off the pretense and so grinds to a sheepish and ignominious halt: "The ingredients necessary to the composition of a moderate portion of that beverage which is peculiarly associated in our minds with the Roast Beef of Old England. I allude to —in short, Punch."

Seeing David after a long interval, Micawber has to recall their last meeting. It was at Canterbury, "Within the shadow, I may figuratively say, of that religious edifice, immortalized by Chaucer, which was anciently the resort of Pilgrims from the remotest corners of—in short . . . in the immediate neighbourhood of the cathedral."

Micawber keeps a formal, elegant tone by using the third person in address instead of the more familiar second, and by avoiding one's first name. Poor little David from the outset is called "my dear Copperfield," like a contemporary in middle age; indeed he often seems older than his preposterous landlord, certainly more in touch with life as it is. But the 18th-century influence seems clearest when Micawber rolls forth an impressive array of abstract terms, often of Latin derivation. Besides the direct use of Latin such as "in statu quo," "in esse . . . in posse," "(D.V.)," we come upon the famous "pressure of pecuniary embarrassments," "salubrity," "the silent monitor," "possessing myself of a cognomen to which I can establish no legitimate pretensions," "a tacitly consenting party," "impiety of the aspiration," "deeply sensible of your cordiality" and many more that lie everywhere on the surface.

Leaving aside the use of Gray's *Elegy* and passages from Burns "the immortal exciseman nurtured beyond the Tweed" which attest to Micawber's more romantic side, he seems fond of Johnson and *The Vanity of Human Wishes*. Micawber refers to the fame of his provincial town which extends "Shall I say from China to Peru?" and one has to think of Johnson's line "Toil, envy, want, the patron and the jail" as the great tragedian laments "I have ever been the sport and toy of debasing circumstances. Ignominy, Want, Despair, and Madness, have collectively or separately, been the attendants of my career."

Until we have a full study of the imagery of Dickens, we may settle for enough of Micawber's verbal luxury to show its energy and range. Himself a work of literary art, Micawber is a man of letters who sees life in poetic terms. His figurative language applies to the situation that calls it forth, and is inseparable from his character as a whole. Indeed most of Dickens' amiable frauds are heavily metaphorical, and Micawber is presented in terms that bring out his avoidance of actual life. To himself, Micawber's metaphors are like his I O U's; they are as good as the fact, and enable him to escape actually paying money or actually suffering beyond the moment. The I O U's are one side of the poetry of Micawberism, figures of speech for payment, and to their author more real than actual payment could ever be.

Micawber can let himself go and range widely in search of the figures needed to suggest his view of life and experience. He is especially fond of the sea; of the sun, sky, and horizon; of religious altars and other sacred associations; of sports or athletic actions, mythological allusions; of the earth and its cultivation; indeed of the myriad operations of nature so endlessly adaptable to poetic uses.

But Micawber's images of disaster show the happiest union of form and content, the clear necessity in his character to free himself from trouble through its metaphorical expression. He is a "foundered bark," "hope has sunk beneath the horizon," "the bolt is impending and the tree must fall," "one gleam of day might . . . penetrate into the cheerless dungeon of his remaining existence," he is "a waif and stray upon the shore of human nature," "a smouldering volcano long suppressed," "the die is cast—all is over" and he hides "the ravages of care with a sickly mask of mirth," he is, if allowed to cull "a figure of speech from the vocabulary of our coarser national sport . . . forever floored," "The canker is in the flower. The cup is bitter to the brim. The worm is at his work" and his "course is run." "The fair land of promise lately looming on the horizon is again enveloped in impenetrable mists, and forever withdrawn from the eyes of a drifting wretch whose doom is sealed." The God of day has vanished and clouds again are descending upon the dreary scene so that it is indeed "a work of supererogation to add that dust and ashes are for ever scattered on the head of Wilkins Micawber."

The implied reference to the bitter cup of Gethsemane that no man may refuse from his divine father, and Micawber's use of the passage where Job repents amid dust and ashes before the presence of God—all this adds new grandeur to his rhetoric. Now he and his difficulties are one with the timeless agony of mankind and its universal expression in the Bible itself. Dust and ashes are forever scattered on the head of one who likewise has been unable to solve the problems of inexplicable suffering and evil visited upon a superior and just man for whom nothing seems willing to turn up, and who therefore has no choice but to bow his head beneath a shower of these symbols of earthly ruin and its lamentation.

Still, human greatness is not to be defeated. Soaring above all misery on the wings of metaphor, this tremendous fool can welcome the very specters that long have menaced him and his family. When "mutual confidence" has been restored between himself and his loyal wife, Micawber cries out an ecstatic greeting to the worst that life can array against him.

"Now welcome poverty!" cried Mr. Micawber, shedding tears. "Welcome misery, welcome houselessness, welcome hunger, rags, tempest, and beggary! Mutual confidence will sustain us to the end!"

The problems of life are met with the same abstractions as always, and the specters are routed in their own terms. The fact is defeated by the word, the menace is banished by a metaphor, and poverty becomes only a word or a notion, not an affair of food and clothing. So the great optimist cries defiance to this "variety of bleak prospects" and calls upon his wife and family to come forth and sing a chorus.

Alas, however, the chorus can not proceed, "Mrs. Micawber having, in the strength of her emotions, fainted away." In the shadow of her great husband this rare creature has been obscured from our view, and now before we read further, we should help to revive her from the swoon into which she has naturally fallen, while we are mindful of that consideration which her delicacy demands. For Mrs. Micawber is a woman of gentle upbringing who breathes an air of refinement, as of one unused to the distress under which her husband might temporarily suffer—a wife of unswerving loyalty, a woman of remarkable intellectual capacities which enable her not only to understand with unusual clearness and logic the facts of business and economy, but to rise above passing embarrassments with disdainful ease.

Her very first remark to David establishes the tone of Emma's character. Never had it crossed her mind that she would be reduced to accepting a lodger. After all, when she lived with papa and mama, and when she had access to that grand abstraction, her family, with all of its many branches and their vast resources, the larder of which she was then accustomed to speak with its fullness in contrast to an ever-present emptiness—when this was available to her, little did she dream of such an extremity.

As David says, "This was the strain in which she began, and she went on accordingly all the time I knew her."

She had to seem part of an impressive, stable group that had some size and importance, whose views must be taken into account in any effort to solve Mr. Micawber's difficulties. After an exasperating series of impositions, borrowings, and explanations patiently endured, the family in all its branches seemed to develop a cool attitude, especially when threatened by a new pecuniary bite. But no matter even if things had to be pawned, Mrs. Micawber would be genteel. With her vivid recollections of "papa and mama," such transactions must seem very painful and, if they now become necessary, let them at least be carried out on the highest social level allowed by the circumstances. When Micawber's library had to be sold, the affair must not be entrusted to Clickett; she "being of a vulgar mind, would take painful liberties if so much confidence was reposed in her. Master Copperfield, if I might ask you. . . ." Class distinctions are observed even as one descends to beggary; the humiliating question must be asked with proper gentility, and the tone must never suggest the actual morbidness of the moment.

In her ladylike delicacy and refined sensibility, Mrs. Micawber now and then gives way to her emotions.

David reports that she was in tears or shed tears or dropped a tear "on the twin in hand"; the cool judgment of a French critic M. Monod finds her behavior in bad taste, and her lachrymose recital of troubles from the death of her father to the difficulties of her husband so conventional and even mechanical that Dickens seems to be inviting more our derision than our pity. But this tone is one rather of fond regret or affection at the very moment when the greatest absurdities are reported. It simply turns out that Mrs. Micawber weeps and faints a great deal and Dickens is no more annoyed by this than by other weaknesses of the female condition.

As for the swoon in the lives of women, Dickens finds in the combat between Miss Tox and Mrs. Chick in *Dombey and Son* a lack of that concern which binds the daughters of Eve one to another. When Miss Tox declined into a horizontal position, Mrs. Chick displayed "none of that freemasonry in fainting, by which they are generally bound together in a mysterious bond of sisterhood." Then too Mrs. Susannah Sanders testified at Mr. Pickwick's trial that on at least one occasion in life a swoon must be simply automatic. Like Mrs. Bardell when Pickwick had asked her to "name the day," Mrs. Sanders had fainted away "stone dead when Mr. Sanders asked *her* to name the day, and believed that everybody as called herself a lady would do the same, under similar circumstance."

We can hardly blame Mrs. Micawber then for sharing the common delicacy of all ladies; we must agree sympathetically when she awakens from her last swoon and observes that "the removal of the late misunderstanding between Mr. Micawber and myself was at first too much for me." Of course it was.

If we accept her fragility, however, as appropriate to her sex and gentle birth, what shall we say of her strength and clearness of mind? Gissing makes a famous remark about Mrs. Nickleby that "she puts forth a wonderful luxuriance of amiable fatuity." This must never be said of one who, in her husband's tribute, was "so long the partner of my various vicissitudes, and a woman of remarkable lucidity of intellect."

As Micawber obscures an awkward fact by metaphorical language, his wife escapes the truth by clearness in stating it, by abstract terminology, by reason and analysis, and by an elevated indifference to the absurd ambiguities that arise between her terms and the facts to which they apply. Her logic and firmness discard all non-essentials, until there can be no question as to where the truth lies. That it lies for us in a realm sadly removed from where Mrs. Micawber sees it makes no difference to her whatever.

She loves to refer to her husband's "talent," his "spirit," "mind," "fertile resources," his "abilities" endlessly repeated, and the need of turning his "attention" to "coals" as if he had any attention or as if it were now fixed on anything at all, so as to be obliged to turn toward anything else. The expression "coals" also carries just the right degree of high abstraction, suggesting the vast energies of nature which now are to receive their proper release and exploitation. She never sees the ambiguity of any reference to Mr. Micawber's abilities, nor that any reference to his abilities only shows his lack of them, his failure to use them for any good purpose, or his possession of abilities in the last degree futile.

Similarly she obscures immediate disaster by constant reference to "Mr. Micawber's difficulties," always referring to him in the third person with the title "Mr." as one high in life and demanding a formal address, always covering up the most sordid humiliations by a vague word for something made to seem temporary and easily removed, never using such gross or final terms from whose meaning there can be no escape as ridiculous windbag, incompetent weakling, or plain bankrupt.

So if nothing is ever quite called by its name Mrs. Micawber can be sure that the time has come for her husband to "exert himself, and . . . assert himself." A clear analysis can be made, various possibilities can be reviewed, the economic situation can be assessed, all antagonists can be put clearly in the wrong, and her mind can leap with ease over the intervening steps that separate her husband from the heights to which he is so clearly destined.

When Micawber begins as confidential clerk to Uriah Heep, it follows that he should anticipate becoming a judge. In his own view, his baldness prefigures a judicial calling. Does it not naturally go with a profession that requires a wig? This is a much better reason for his elevation to the bench than any brought forward by his wife. Being a clerk, he must have a judicial mind and so is clearly in line for the bench, "eligible as a Judge or Chancellor." The intervening awkwardness of hard work and experience is omitted; Mrs. Micawber never thinks of the price to be paid for anything, from dinner and rent to distinction in the world. Money is the one stage in reasoning that is always left out; she is the victim of her own clearness and quickness of mind which leaps over the obstacles to solution. Her logic goes straight to the goal, leaving out all impediments to success.

Opposition is in the wrong, and by unassailable logic

things are discarded as unreliable, showing their own weakness on the one hand, with their perpetual doom to mediocrity on the other for having failed to employ Micawber's services. Not coals, not corn, not anything on commission, not banking, not brewing, not alas, after years of exploitation, her "family" in all its manifold "branches"—none of these is to be relied on, so "again I contend that we are no further advanced than we were before." Therefore, "what is the use" of these broken reeds, the fault clearly lying in them although whatever "use" they might have had clearly was beyond the one complaining. Everything, no matter how obvious, is announced as a discovery, and every time Micawber is discussed his wife launches into her familiar strain as if for the first time, until finally she lays the responsibility for the general failure to take advantage of a great man's abilities where, in her view, it belongs—upon society itself before which the "gauntlet" of an advertisement in all the papers is now to be thrown.

So down goes the gauntlet and forward goes the leap, and once more expression has triumphed over fact. We see that Emma's genius lies also in expression, in concept and intellectual grasp but never in active solution. As Micawber makes things disappear by words and phrases, she disposes of them by analysis and logic. Once more it is the literary statement of things that enables the Micawbers to escape the consequences of their behavior. Through it all Emma's loyalty is unshaken. Even though her husband has "misled" her as to certain payments, has "given a bill without consulting me," has "kept me in the dark," has been "improvident" and even "may have concealed his difficulties from me in the first instance"—in short, even though he has lied to her from the outset—the fact remains that "I never will desert Mr. Micawber. It's of no use asking me."

Gissing shows that Dickens abounds in women who are the curse of their husband's lives. Mrs. Snagsby, Mrs. Bumble, Mrs. Varden, Mrs. Jellyby, Mrs. MacStinger, Mrs. Joe Gargery, Mrs. Pocket come readily to mind, but Emma Micawber is not among them. Belligerent as these other ladies sometimes are against their lords, Mrs. Micawber for her part abuses anyone who might suppose that she could desert her husband; she is warlike on his behalf as called for by her marriage vows. Like Mrs. Gamp who created an imaginary friend and supporter, Mrs. Harris, to bolster the weakness of her position, Mrs. Micawber to display her own fortitude has invented an opposition to which no name is ever given but which looms as fierce and militant, constantly demanding something, or threatening a course of action against which Emma will stand no matter what the odds. "It is no use" for this nameless antagonist to ask her—she never will desert . . . although no one has ever thought of asking her to do that or anything like it. She repeats a series of arguments that no one would dream of opposing, and so displays her firmness, her superb logic, her absolute fidelity—admirable virtues all, yet all beside the point or rather above it with a kind of Olympian irrelevance.

If Mrs. Micawber's fidelity is militant and her acceptance of the marriage final, only rarely does her great husband drop a hint that he longs for the days of his freedom. If he expected more from her family he should have had the foresight of the great Mr. Bumble in *Oliver Twist* who, while contemplating a proposal to the beauteous Mrs. Corney, took advantage of her absence from the room to count the silver, assess the furniture, search the chest of drawers, shake a small padlock box and, hearing therefrom a pleasant sound like the clinking of coin, determined that his liberty would not be surrendered in vain and said gravely, "I'll do it!"

At any rate, Micawber found himself repulsed in the course of time, and the family even went so far as to "express their dissatisfaction" on hearing that Mrs. Micawber was to have another baby, and finally to repudiate the Micawbers entirely after a cool reception and various personal remarks. Mrs. Micawber's constant efforts at reconciliation, at persuading "the Lion" to lie down "with the lamb" without specifying which was which—these efforts came to nothing for a long time and were finally traced "to an apprehension . . . that Mr. Micawber would require pecuniary accommodation." The family refused to waste another cent, and in the light of a disillusionment so unexpected and unreasonable for a great man to endure, we cannot blame Micawber if he let fall a sigh to David in recalling the period "when I was myself in a state of celibacy, and Mrs. Micawber had not yet been solicited to plight her faith at the Hymeneal altar." He had been in difficulties ever since.

But Micawber never can regret anything for long, even though one might say that Emma's fidelity increases the difficulties which it is part of her genius to lament. Mrs. Micawber will not desert her husband, but she will do nothing more for him either. Neither her logic nor fidelity achieves anything practical, but only increases Micawber's trials. So we must ask for whose benefit but her own is this irrelevant devotion insisted on? She never suggests that Micawber might desert her. She alone seems to have good reason for desertion, and assumes that he has none to leave her. In this way she conceals her need of him beneath a claim of virtue in not deserting him.

All the valor, however, is not on her side since she could not exist without him and needs him desperately. Dickens reveals Emma by a fine touch in her anxiety before Micawber exposes Heep. She learns that her husband is going to London, and writes to Traddles with her same absurd inflation of words and unconscious humor, so that we laugh at the ridiculous expression of a pathetically genuine feeling. She finds out Micawber's destination from the direction-card attached to "the little brown valise of happier days" whereon "the eagle-glance of matrimonial anxiety detected d,o,n, distinctly traced." After all, this must be counted a successful marriage, and when Micawber sails for Australia his devoted wife is with him, vowing fidelity as always. It is often said that David's own marriage is a failure; that of the Micawbers can never end.

Dickens' public reading of Mrs. Micawber was another triumph. Somehow he was able to draw the lines of her character into an impression of final rightness, which followed from her unanswerable logic as she steadily reasoned all other forces into the wrong. He presented her sipping hot punch, smoothing her hair, and discussing the prospects of her husband. She gave her personal view of the marital obligations assumed upon her union with Micawber. On the night preceding, she had read over the marriage service by her bedroom candle. The terms then reviewed forced her to conclude that she must never desert Mr. Micawber.

Dickens had an irresistible way of showing her triumphant championship of the obvious as if it were her personal discovery, and he could put her in the right about things that no one else ever thought of questioning, as if it all had been a great achievement. He pictured her determined stand against all opposition, and her majestic conquest of society as the gauntlet was cast down and the one who would take it up was challenged now to step forward.

It is no fault of Emma's that the party does not come forward, unless perhaps she has terrified the party by the lucidity of her reasoning, by the incontrovertible solution at which her genius has arrived. The world is then exposed for what it is and human affairs must limp forward as best they can; Micawber's difficulties vanish when Emma proves how responsible the world is for them, and the great pair stride upward into their immortality.

Mr. Micawber's Abilities

As Mr. Cockshut would agree, such poets and actors do not need our help, and gain little from attempts to make them seem clearer. But we have an excuse for not yet leaving them, in a number of questions often repeated. Has Dickens made a mistake in presenting Micawber too sympathetically when, according to George Orwell, he is nothing but a "cadging scoundrel"? Is it out of character to show Micawber as the conqueror of Heep and the shrewd detector of his villainy? Finally is it wrong to send the Micawbers to Australia, where the former incompetent turns into an industrious man who pays his debts and rises to high social position?

Now if we are amused at Micawber's ludicrous pretensions, our response often shades into anger at what in actual life would be plain dishonesty. Is he in fact a half-criminal nuisance or just a harmless incompetent unsuited to the problems of life? He can be enjoyed, to be sure, as the comic literary type of beloved rascal, similar to the Falstaff whom he resembles.

Yet Micawber has been charged with knowing just what he is about, with preaching what he has no intention of carrying out in fact, with being unworthy of our affection because he has swindled honest men like Traddles. He is a dangerous hypocrite, then, especially after the Traddles episode, and Dickens has made a mistake in changing him from his original harmless absurdity. David warns his friend Traddles against lending Micawber any money, although he seems not to "mean any harm, poor fellow." On hearing that a bill of Micawber's has been signed, however, David hopes "there will be nothing wrong about it."

Does this mean that David considers Micawber dishonest, or only as someone innocent and foolish? Again, why is it that Micawber never tries to borrow money from David when they meet again, and the "companion of my youth" is on his way to mature success? Does this suggest that Micawber knows he will never pay anyone back and prefers not to cheat an old friend? Is he having compassion on his old boy-lodger, as David suggests, deciding that he will impose only on strangers or on Mrs. Micawber's family, his natural prey? Does Micawber, in short, know that he is playing a mean trick on anyone he borrows from?

The answer must lie again in expression, in metaphor, in believing that the utterance of a thing removes any problem in it. Eventually Micawber makes his peace with Traddles and his own conscience. "I beg to hand to my friend Mr. Thomas Traddles my I O U" for a specific sum, replacing two sets of worthless paper with one. David observes that "this was quite the same to Mr. Micawber as paying the money"; Traddles himself falls under the spell and imagines that he is adequately paid.

Still Gissing maintains that Micawber is sincere by his lights; he really does think that something will turn up so that he can pay the bill that Traddles, also sure that Micawber would pay if he could, finds on his hands. Even though Micawber can give his famous economic advice about living within one's income he is led astray by his own words and imagination. In jail he borrows a shilling from little David. "He gave me a written order on Mrs. Micawber for the amount, and put away his pocket-handkerchief, and cheered up."

Micawber cheers up not because he has the money or ever will have it to pay back. It is making the gesture, acting like one who has the money. This is enough, and illusion is more real to him than the fact would be. The order for a shilling is the more absurd for its being written; not only does the writing emphasize the worthlessness of what is promised, it is sent for payment to one who has even less to pay with than Micawber himself. His sense of virtue and integrity always increases whenever he has written down his obligations and signed an acknowledgment of them. All of his satisfactions of debt rest on similar nothingness. So long as the I O U is worthless, Micawber will be happy.

Nothing in his life must have any reality or substance except his troubles. In moments of self-depreciation it occurs to him that he occupies "another man's place in existence" in vain, but this is not the same as admitting to outright dishonesty. After all, as Traddles points out after the Heep disclosures, Micawber seems to have done "right for right's sake, when we reflect what terms he might have made with Uriah Heep himself, for silence."

Thus he was able to expose the dishonesty of Heep without realizing his own nearness to outright fraud. To the very end everyone accepted Micawber's belief in his signed agreements to pay; it is the special peculiarity of an amiable weakling, something to be indulged because it so clearly made him feel better while no one ever thought of being paid back. It was agreed that the family should be outfitted, their passage to Australia paid, and a hundred pounds provided, "and that Mr. Micawber's arrangement for the repayment of the advances should be gravely entered into, as it might be wholesome for him to suppose himself under that responsibility."

Again such an arrangement seems proper in *David Copperfield* where people can afford to excuse a comic spendthrift. They all see that the exact figuring of his debt gives Micawber the greatest delight, as if the fact of doing so were the main thing. Making clear to the penny just how much he owes is better than not knowing how much it is that he can never repay. Is it not a greater satisfaction to pay a large debt than a small one? To Micawber, the bigger the sum, the greater the joy in agreeing to pay it, what counts really being the knowledge, the resolution, the intention and promise to pay, the making out of exact sums, and the composing of formal documents. When this is done he has in effect paid the debt and restored his dignity, not seeing any connection between the clearness of the debt and the need of paying it.

So, just before his emigration, Micawber draws up a fantastic catalog of sums, the like of which David has never seen outside of a school ciphering-book, detailing the compound interest on his debt which he figures can be paid in two years, fifteen calendar months, and fourteen days from that date. To discharge all this he gives a note-of-hand beautifully neat, and is serenely happy.

So Dickens' sympathy for Micawber keeps within Micawber's world, while he knows perfectly well how close Micawber might come to being a scoundrel past any tolerance. He enjoys the gayety and self-deception, the pretentious façade of his creation; but if Micawber were dishonest Dickens would not see anything funny in his not paying people what he owes them. Micawber is absurd in being totally unable to perform what he says or professes. This is the Micawberism in all of us, and Dickens makes it extremely funny while leaving us with a sense that Micawber has redeemed himself from his I O U's by his unconscious picture of the absurdity in us all.

Besides, if Dickens had intended us to sit in sterner judgment on Micawber, he could easily have found in him more of Montagu Tigg or Harold Skimpole. Like Traddles, poor Tom Pinch in *Martin Chuzzlewit* is asked for a loan. But Tigg is clearly a rascal, and the more extreme his promises to repay the more obvious his dishonesty. In both Micawber and Tigg we know that the money never will be repaid, yet one is obviously a villain and the other is not. Chesterton insists that Dickens wishes us to like Micawber and to think of him in the end as harmless. The standard comparison with Harold Skimpole in *Bleak House* and the father of *Little Dorrit* proves his point. Aside from the malice against Leigh Hunt, Skimpole shows "the dark underside of Micawber," the dangerous, unforgivable element in all pretentious frauds—in short, all that is left out of Micawber or at least outweighed by our enjoyment.

Skimpole pretends a total weakness and ignorance when money is called for. He is a drone who will enjoy life sustained by the labor of others. Skimpole says, "I really mean the money without paying it," and is casual, matter-of-fact; there are no metaphors in this bankrupt and hence no redemption. He does not really care about his debts, does not really think of paying for anything. He claims to be a child, knowing nothing of time and money, nothing of responsibility or principle. Micawber, for all of the inflated nonsense of his talk, would like nothing so much as to assume great responsibility, to be active in affairs and business. He thinks constantly of his debts and pays them in the only coin he has—in the poetry of his I O U's. Where Skimpole is a monstrosity of egotism and selfishness, Micawber is affectionate and loyal—a fool of any dimensions, if you will, but never a cynical parasite.

Finally, there is "Micawber in defeat" if William Dorrit is the logical end of a hopeless insolvent. Micawber and Dorrit both find themselves in jail, and perhaps Dorrit is only what Micawber must have become in actual life. But in Micawber's world jail provides the happiest episode; he is not weak and beaten, but full of joy and defiance. Micawber likes jail and is not ashamed of having been there, sentiments unlike the embarrassing snobbery and self-deception of Dorrit.

Selfish and ungrateful, Dorrit offends us by insensitive exploitation of his daughter, as if her sacrifice were only his due in return for the services he has rendered in keeping up the family's tone and appearance; if he let himself be aware that a sacrifice is being made, he would not let the poor child know that he knew, but would choose to pretend that such sacrifice was needless and uncalled for. His attitude forces her to conceal the truth and to go on with her self-immolation.

Dorrit is a spectacle of whining, degenerate self-pity; together with Harold Skimpole, he suggests in Dickens an attitude of unrelieved contempt. There is nothing really funny about either of them, nothing therefore to inspire the sympathy and tolerance that Dickens asks for Micawber. After such a comparison we see what Dickens would have done had he desired us to condemn Micawber as an outright scoundrel. After Skimpole and William Dorrit we have no lasting objection to Micawber's unprovided bills. Indeed, how could we have been so impertinent as to speak of dishonesty, or to demand a thing like money from one already giving us more than we can absorb of his own inexhaustible riches?

A further objection holds that Dickens involves the great comic creations too deeply in his plots, making them act through the story in ways that contradict their real nature. So the entire relationship with Heep becomes forced and outlandish, opposed to Micawber's general ineptitude and vagueness. It is said that Heep would not employ such a good-for-nothing as Micawber, who could never have done the work required. It is all too systematic, planned, and controlled to be in character. Micawber never has shown any of these qualities before and is now forced into them by the plot —and what is a plot that it should distort the nature of so great a man?

An opposite view is taken by those who agree with E. K. Brown, wherein it is entirely natural for Micawber, a good man, to expose an evil one. According to the "Carol Philosophy" of Dickens, the evil were no match for the good, while simple and honest men were certain to overcome intelligent knaves. So, on the contrary, it is just such a man as Micawber who should expose such a creature as Heep, and to reason otherwise is to reason from outside of Dickens' world and its assumptions.

How immediate this problem seems, how important it is to decide what we think about it, to take sides in a debate carried on fiercely as if dealing with an objective reality! Both sides are right; Micawber's role in exposing Heep somewhat contradicts his usual futility, but it offers a new example of his energy when he is working for others with no benefit to himself. His honesty emerges, or at least a lively sense of fraud in others.

Micawber's relationship with Heep begins in chapter seventeen, where the villain hears, much to David's embarrassment, of Micawber's difficulties. Presumably Heep then decides to use this needy individual in his plot against Wickfield, assuming that he can easily be blackmailed once he is in economic bondage to Heep. Micawber will become involved in the whole corruption with no one any the wiser. Or, the design to use Micawber may in fact have started to Heep's mind on seeing the famous advertisement, the gauntlet thrown down to society. This seems to be Micawber's own view, since in his letter of exposure he refers to his meagre salary of twenty-two shillings and six per week, which has forced him to borrow money to support a "blighted but rising family."

Of course this "necessity had been foreseen by Heep" who secured the loans with Micawber's I O U's, installed him as tenant in his old house, so that like the innocent ones in *Othello,* Micawber "became enmeshed in the web he had spun for my reception." At first, Micawber had no idea that he was being trapped. The gauntlet had been taken up by "my friend Heep" who is of course "a man of remarkable shrewdness" certain to become attorney general.

Heep is indeed shrewd and, while he sees what Micawber's chief weaknesses are, he seems again, like Iago, to underestimate the resourcefulness of decent human beings and to exaggerate his own cleverness, blinded as he is by ambition, resentment, and contemptuous superiority. His view of Micawber naturally follows. As reported by the great man himself Heep has told him that, without the position in his office, Micawber would probably be a "mountebank about the country, swallowing a sword-blade, and eating the devouring element," in short, a freak in a traveling side show. When the exposure begins Heep refers to Micawber as "a dissipated fellow" and "my clerk, who is the very scum of society."

Heep has simply taken on someone as a tool whom he despises; his opinion and use of Micawber then are not widely out of character. So also Micawber's acceptance of a job with Heep, his failure to see through him at first, his becoming enmeshed, as he says, is part of his own hopeless inability to do anything right for himself and his family. As Micawber says, he has had a good deal to do with the law "as a defendant on civil process" and his very baldness assures an eventual appointment to the bench. Micawber's working regularity is no doubt absurd, but his employment with Heep and his attitude toward it is no more outlandish than anything profitable he might try to do. Any regular job would of course have grandiose possibilities; his imagination would clothe it with splendor at first, and Mrs. Micawber would leave out the awkward intervening steps toward greatness from any beginning.

But we should go further and praise Micawber's honesty along with his labor for the benefit of others. In spite of his nonsense and windy evasions of debt and responsibility, Micawber is genuinely shocked at Heep's villainy. It may be out of his character to plan in secret for a long time the eventual unmasking of Heep, to accumulate shrewdly a mass of evidence, to behave, that is, with unprecedented foresight. But he is consistent in resolving that he will not go on aiding the dishonesty of Heep, and his method of writing an enormous letter to be read aloud while threatening the culprit with a ruler is a triumphant return to the essence of his character.

In sorrowing outrage he runs through the vocabulary of denunciation, first in London and then at the final oration. Heep is a forger, cheat, liar, serpent, abandoned rascal, transcendent and immoral hypocrite and perjurer who has deliberately engaged in deception, fraud, conspiracy, and all manner of baseness in a wicked attempt to ruin Wickfield who "has been for years deluded and plundered in every conceivable manner, to the pecuniary aggrandisement of the avaricious, false, and grasping—Heep," the whole monstrous affair perpetuated "by a miscellaneous catalogue of unscrupulous chicaneries." True, here is more of the rhetoric so dear to Micawber's heart, another escape from disaster in its exaggerated expression; the fact remains that Heep's criminality has shaken Micawber to the soul, and he responds as would any decent person. To this extent the so-called "Carol Philosophy" of Dickens transforms a bungling incompetent into a sober and efficient man.

But we come back to the one flaw in Micawber's otherwise boundless ineptitude. He is a zealous friend able to work hard for others. David remarks on this trait when Micawber is in jail and when things go wrong at his famous dinner party. When the arrangements collapse, Micawber takes over and rescues the entire evening by his gayety and energy, transforming the disastrous leg of mutton into deliciously crisp slices, restoring the general appetite, directing the whole exercise with complete assurance and success.

We have already seen him in jail, a great authority in the club formed among the debtors, proposing the formal request to Parliament for a change in the law of imprisonment for debt, drawing up "on an immense sheet of paper" the petition itself which cannot possibly do any good beyond pleasing the author's vanity and calling attention to his difficulties. David's comment on the petition already quoted reminds us of the best defense for Micawber's exposure of Heep. Here are satisfied at least two Micawberesque conditions established early in his portrait; he can write a long letter which gets rid of his trouble through words, and he can play a role in something that is less beneficial to himself than to others.

"I wonder," Aunt Betsey observes, "you have never turned your thoughts to emigration." Aunt Betsey adds her intention to advance the needed capital, and in no time at all the Australian expedition is under way. Opinion is again sharply divided. J. B. Priestley and Somerset Maugham see nothing out of the way in Micawber's Australian triumphs, whereas Chesterton and Quiller-Couch are strongly opposed.

Ignoring the private attitude of Dickens himself toward emigration we must divide our approval once more. Surely the idea of sending Micawber to Australia is beyond praise as a comic device, drawing together as it does the essential features of both the Micawbers. Their preparations for departure and Emma's comment on what her husband may expect to become in a new nation are a riot of the preposterous. But the report of Micawber's reform, his new capacity for hard work, the repayment of his debts, and his achievement of respectability are simply deplorable. Here is a side of Dickens which devoted readers must accept in embarrassed silence.

Australia is on the other side of the world, yet imagination soon carries Micawber there and he behaves like a vigorous and intrepid pioneer. Everything has to be something other than what it is; and David remarks that it is odd but "wonderfully like Mr. Micawber, that when he went from London to Canterbury he should have talked as if he were going to the farthest limits of the earth, and when he went from England to Australia as if he were going for a little trip across the Channel." Now the entire family are assigned to various Australian tasks; they must be prepared for the rigors of a frontier existence, must accept their lot as "denizens of the forest" who give up the luxuries of England and renounce "the refinements of the land of the free." The younger children observe the habits of pigs and poultry in lower-class districts, the great man himself turns his attention to the arts of baking! The eldest daughter gets up at five in the morning to learn how to milk cows, and Wilkins, Jr. issues forth with a walking stick to practice the driving of cattle. That the young ones are nearly killed by being run over and Wilkins, Jr. driven off with imprecations from the cattle herders only gives zest to Micawber's defiance of actual life.

Finally, on board ship, he is the perfect frontiersman, a child of the wilderness, returning to native haunts. His air is bold, alert, and confident, his preparations for a sea voyage more professional than those of Mr. Peggotty himself. He wears a kind of oilskin suit, with a low straw hat on his head. Carrying a mariner's telescope under his arm, he casts his eye shrewdly up at the sky, on the lookout for dirty weather, as indeed he should be. Mrs. Micawber and all the children are similarly done up "like preserved meats, in impervious cases."

All this aims to resist the coming storms, and the

whole absurd picture shows again Micawber's inability to do anything sensible on his own behalf, his literally not knowing how to come in out of the rain and stay out of it, while loading himself down with useless protection. Similarly when making punch Micawber peels the lemons with a clasp-knife about a foot long which he wipes on his coatsleeve, while the children all have wooden spoons attached to their bodies—everything very rough and homespun down to a series of "villainous little tin pots" out of which everyone had to drink punch when a good supply of glasses was right on hand.

Micawber's getting ready for one of his springs is like the aging Coleridge of Carlyle's fierce portrait. When preparing an argument, Coleridge would amass "logical swimbladders, transcendental life-preservers, and all manner of precautionary and vehiculatory gear before setting out." Like Micawber, Coleridge thought of answering a question as if he were embarking on a long journey, the preparations for which consumed more energy and trouble than the voyage itself.

And nowadays is not Micawber everywhere in the "Do-it-yourself movement"? Instead of just coming in out of the rain and wind, the pioneer encumbers himself with a grotesque apparatus of self-protection. Like the intense householder bent on saving money, he wastes his resources to save them. Vast trouble is taken to avoid the cost of having work done by someone whose business it is to do it. The machinery for action becomes an end in itself, getting ready is the main thing. There is great expense for tools and materials, time and money disappear into inferior work which has to be redone at more expense and trouble, nothing really works, and the result is one of a thousand daily facets of essential Micawberism—a mass of futility behind a great façade.

But Mrs. Micawber is soberly logical in reviewing chances for distinction in Australia. One discovery after another is announced as if no one had ever thought of it, all befitting a practical woman who will not evade the facts and their implications. The main question is, can Australia provide adequate scope for a man of Mr. Micawber's peculiar abilities?

With his comic invention never better, Dickens gives Emma a wide-open language in keeping with endless vistas in the new continent; her mind leaps with agility over the obstructions between Micawber's arrival and his ascent into the governor's mansion. Her terms are of expanding, rising, developing, and ranging, Mr. Micawber's abilities being those "peculiarly requiring space" —all with her usual solemn unconsciousness of absurdity: indeed his abilities do require space, consisting mostly of wind requiring an unconfined area to blow in.

But the ecstatic pair reach a new summit of nonsense in disposing of the fortune soon to be won in Australia. Typically, the fortune is spent before it is obtained. The problem is, ought England to share in that "eminence and fortune" of the Micawbers although, having given Mr. Micawber birth, England has failed to give him employment?

The family view here is disunited, but by her realism and logic Mrs. Micawber prevails: Britannia is not excluded from the wealth of her distinguished son. Micawber at first believes that "Britannia must take her chance" in the future; he feels under no obligation to enrich a country so long insensitive to his genius.

But Emma gradually wears him down, with arguments and facts. Micawber does not realize his own power nor appreciate his position, and he should plan to strengthen, not to weaken, the tie with Albion. He should take his stand on the vessel's prow and cry out that he has come to be "The Caesar of his own fortunes," that he claims as his own the honors, riches, and "posts of profitable pecuniary emolument" in Australia, that he has done with delay and disappointment.

Becoming then an important public character abroad, Mr. Micawber will show his influence at home. Wielding "the rod of talent and of power," he must end as a "page of History," a man to be reckoned with by the sheer magnitude of his shadow.

After a relentless parade of facts and the conclusions they force upon his mind, Mr. Micawber humbly defers to the good sense of his wife. After all, "What will be, will be. Heaven forbid that I should grudge my native country any portion of the wealth that may be accumulated by our descendants." So the plan is to make money and ascend rapidly to high places; then a return to England, to live there that Albion may share in her children's greatness.

Surely no one would wish to give up these pages, as the saying is. Dickens' sense of drollery is inexhaustible here, and beyond anything in *David Copperfield* the vision of Australia is preposterous. The illusion and maladjustment to reality are never more absurd. The Micawbers have learned nothing from experience; hardly a syllable of their riotous discourse is not deluded or wide of the mark and they go on like children into a new world unchanged from what has defeated them in the old. And just this sense, that they have not really changed, forces rejection of Dickens' final report from Australia. Here is an unforgivable distortion of Micawber's nature that we can never accept. He should never have worked for profit to pay his debts; indeed it should never have crossed his mind that the debts were still to be paid.

Granted that many of Micawber's qualities were bound to find their setting in Australia. A new colony requires optimistic people. Micawber needs the scope and space of a great open land to develop his views and abilities, as the land itself needs his resilience and buoyancy. Then too, his fine presence and distinguished manner would be certain to thrive in a vast, thinly settled country, calling on personalities of great dimensions to fill it out.

Further, his talents as a writer would find release; Forster is right to wonder that Micawber had never taken up journalism in England. He is writing all the time, and as a newspaper correspondent in Australia, composing letters at every opportunity and planning to bring out a volume of selections, he seems engaged in the one occupation at which he might succeed without violence to his character. Certainly Micawber's great phrases and the swollen rhetoric of his hopes and romantic dreams would be right for a pioneering press. Inspiring slogans, eloquent and invincible faith in the colony's future, uplifting energy and assurance—these precede the conquest of great empires. So while others did the actual work Micawber might become a spiritual force, carrying onward the despondent, revitalizing the faint of heart, brushing aside the discouragements and obstacles before all great enterprises, inspiring the doubtful and timid by his vision of success, and turning by the force of his genius the most profound despair into a buoyant hope.

Again, Micawber as a magistrate or some kind of public official does not contradict the man who sails to Australia. Since Micawber is useful only for the benefit of others, he might well become a public hero deserving a testimonial dinner at which he gives a magnificently ornate address reported by himself to the newspapers, the climax of which is the sound advice never to owe more than you can pay. So long as it is mostly talk with no steady activity in business, Micawber might well be assigned to a career of public service at any one of many levels. He might succeed in charitable foundations or uplift work, but never in private-enterprise economics. We prefer to think of him in activities like the Salvation Army or community chest, in great fund-raising campaigns for noble causes largely based on promises to pay gradually or in the future, but never in the steady increments of business.

So we might believe reports of Micawber in Australian journalism or public service making use of his eloquence. That he labors in the bush until his bald head, perspiring in the sun has almost "melted away," and that he has paid all his debts—these things cannot be true. We must agree that Micawber is a success only while he is a failure; after all, many people do well in life and no one thinks anything of it. Only Micawber is immortal through failure, so it must be that Dickens was misinformed.

Micawber did not become something other than what he really was, so Dickens was clearly the victim of false information. After all, bulletins from across the sea are sometimes unreliable, and the news of Micawber's solvency is an obvious libel against the integrity of a great man. Dickens ought to have checked his sources before accepting the report. In 1941, Mr. J. H. McNulty found himself troubled by many unanswered questions in the reading of Dickens. Among other solutions, he has Mr. Micawber appear in a dream to John Everyman, there to assert that the story of his success in Australia as a magistrate was an absurdity. His talents lay actually in finance, and the fact was that he had gone to Australia but had returned very shortly. He had found it a barbarous place, and we are left with the injunction to "read the novel again and you'll see that I'm right."

This is good advice. It is not enough to say that Dickens desired poetic justice for his absurd friend, and so gave him the chance never offered in England. For Micawber, certainly, the ideal of a Dickens ending is reversed. As Orwell says, the main characters end as a rule in a "sort of radiant idleness," not having to work any more, whereas Micawber who has never done anything is rewarded by finding out how to work, or finding a place where he can work and where the whole idea of his working at all is not ridiculous.

As other good people in Dickens move from work to idleness, so Micawber moves from idleness to work. The immortal bankrupt is transformed into a success; for anyone else, we would say that this was the proper reward. With Micawber it is a blemish on his greatness, because it destroys his mastery of figurative language. He has been a gigantic metaphor himself, overcoming the facts and the need of money in life by expressing them in metaphors of such power and vividness that they disappear. The waiting for something to turn up, the spring, the leap, the gauntlet, the expectation, and the I O U—these are the truth for Micawberism. The whole point of the exact catalog of debts before emigration is that they won't be paid; yet we hear that they are paid and we are disappointed, even shocked. It is a triumph of Dickens' genius that he can make not paying one's debts seem funny in his created universe. But what is funny about payment?

Further, the last letter written by Micawber while still in England has an important reference to the debtors' prison, that secure haven where we saw Micawber at his happiest. Why not consign him to prison where he could go on for years in absolute safety from importunate creditors and rapacious bailiffs, there to imagine anything to please him, never obliged to make his own living in Australia or anywhere else? Or better still, why not leave him on the boat after the tearful farewells? Chapter fifty-seven, "The Emigrants," is the height of comic inspiration; a whole pageant of inspired nonsense unfolds before us.

To leave Micawber on the deck of a ship bound for distant horizons which constantly recede and are never reached, which in turn can be peopled with any world that suits the vanity and self-deception of the beholder —surely this is nearer to his essence than pedestrian labor. Every voyage is a symbol of common illusions, and a long journey on the sea from which Micawber always drew such a wealth of imagery is appropriate for a man who needs space indeed to develop his views. We might then compose whole volumes on Micawber's fate as indeed some have done on the Australian phase. We could enjoy endless vistas of delightful speculation as to events when the clouds were dispersed and the dreary scene had faded before the god of day on the horizon.

But no—Dickens loved Micawber so much that he could not keep the great man in difficulties which were inevitable as long as Micawber remained the grandiloquent windbag that he was. Sending him to Australia was a stroke of genius; making him into a different man after arriving there was a blunder, but one that the same Dickens who thought of Micawber in the first place was bound to make. If we cannot have one without the other, the balance is still in our favor.

Let us end by denying again that Dickens made a mistake in growing too fond of Micawber, that he would have been much funnier and a greater comic creation as a whole with less of our sympathy. And despite the fact that we think it best to tolerate absurdity because of our own share in it, Dickens could attack with such insight and penetration as to make us laugh gleefully when something deserves calculated derision. Everyone interested in Dickens sees that he had it in for authority; he was against official people, routine persons, the stiff, cold, or formal—lawyers, fashionable, self-conscious, and vain types in high places. But Dickens was too generous to do his best work in the harshest satiric terms. He had immense energy and a militant temper, but especially in the early novels he could not escape his human pity, his open-hearted sympathy with life. Of this temper, Micawber is the highest achievement, the likable, even indispensable, idiot.

David has just received a devastating letter, the last communication of course that will ever come from "the beggared outcast" who is about to be arrested when his note-of-hand falls due and who faces certain destruction.

David rushes out in search of the writers of this heart-rending missive. Suddenly he meets the London coach with "Mr. and Mrs. Micawber up behind; Mr. Micawber, the very picture of tranquil enjoyment, smiling at

Mrs. Micawber's conversation, eating walnuts out of a paper bag, with a bottle sticking out of his breast pocket." David was much consoled, and felt on the whole "relieved that they were gone—though I still liked them very much."

Aristocracy and the King of Schnorrers

It is easy to see the comic in blundering ineptitude, leading to total failure; but can one be ridiculous who never makes an unprofitable move, never utters an inept word? Is the reader to accept an equally comic total success after the comic total failure of Micawber? It is the special triumph of Zangwill at this point among examples of sympathetic discernment that he resolves so striking a paradox.

A certain form of comic insight seems more marked in Jews than in other men. Everyone who discusses Jewish humor remarks how the sombreness of this people's history has given a special tone to what it sees as funny. The Jews have loved life certainly; they have a will to endure, to survive when everything is done to make life intolerable for them, when everything is regularly taken away but life itself. We all have to accept the realities no matter how grim they are and laughter through tears is common enough; but this endurance is doubly imposed on the Jews who must accept the repudiation and abuse of other men.

If the comic view of life is needed to help us endure what we see, so is it needed to make things easier and sweeter especially for those who have to suffer at the hands of others. When we think what a monstrous and unspeakable joke has been played on the Jews, we can see why they have developed a rueful comic view the better to endure it. Their humor emerges from a background of sorrow and evil and the need to accept them; one stands such things better by making jokes which give a certain relief and perspective. So the combination joke of Jewish humor comes from having to laugh instead of wailing.

The mother of little Mottel the Cantor's Son so tenderly described by Sholom Aleichem is constantly weeping as a background for the delightful, innocent sweetness of the boy's enjoyment of life. What a long history of abuse lies behind the story of the labor dispute in which certain conditions of work were to be accepted by the employer. Mottel thinks wonderingly that "never before did a worker stipulate exactly how he was to be beaten." Perhaps the blows will not be quite so painful if seen in the right historical perspective!

From death and beggary themselves the Jews have extracted the ludicrous. We will soon meet a dryly amusing fellow, one Yankelé Ben Yitzchok, who makes his living as a beggar. He meets an acquaintance, whose father has recently died. Yankelé wants to be sympathetic, but sees no reason that his profession should not be exercised.

"Ah, yes," said Yankelé chokingly. "Your fader was a great and good man—just my size!"

Later on Yankelé is obliged to beg from the formidable Rabbi Remorse Red Herring, whose profession it is to preach sermons of consolation. The Rabbi has five basic utterances which he can adapt to any occasion, depending on the age, sex, or condition of the deceased. With delightful ambiguity Yankelé says to him, "If you should die, who would console the community?"

This tendency to joke recalls the numerous stories of miracles in Jewish history. Miracles show rescue from defeat, triumph through unexpected reversals of fortune, divine help in hopeless situations. So also the joke that overcomes apparent disaster or defeat at the last minute. The miracle is typical of men facing adversity not to be borne without divine aid; so is the Jewish joke natural for those whose actual lives contain so much agony.

Closely related is the fact that if a Jew resents something he can't do anything about it. He can talk, however, or imagine what he would do if he could. People in exile or otherwise physically helpless cannot defend themselves; hence the Jews are such a convenient object of persecution. But words they have, and a kind of defense by verbose invective, comic exaggeration, and absurd insults which give vent to frustration at other levels.

So the comedy of insult flourishes, especially when there is no chance to carry out a threat in action. As in the scolding of small boys or the barking of little dogs, the noise made is ludicrously out of proportion to the offense first, and secondly to any chance that action will come of it. The greater the noise the greater is the relief to him who makes it, and the less likelihood that it will ever get beyond noise. We hear it said that goodness or virtue is one, but vice and wickedness are multifarious. So the comic resources of malediction are endless and those of praise are limited; it is only praise of oneself that is really comic, because it betrays the greatest of all absurdities—our vanity.

These elementary thoughts about Jewish humor came to mind in the search for some example that would be typical but not too obvious. Freud has included some very amusing jokes in his study of wit, among them a series dealing with the *schnorrer,* a name for what was at one time an accepted institution in the Jewish community, a professional beggar who received the alms that were demanded of everyone as part of one's religious duty. This pathetic, absurd figure was given a kind of literary immortality by Israel Zangwill in a highly amusing book, *The King of Schnorrers* (1893).

Not only do we get some hilarious incongruities here, but we see a form of Jewish humor which so often springs from their tragedy. Leaving aside the lot of common humanity and what it demands of one man toward another, the most preposterous comedy emerges from misery and want. Never mentioned is what these people must have endured in sorrow and exile before the need to beg of one another arose in the first place. Once more these things are inseparable from the Jewish human lot and they are better endured if accepted and treated comically. If begging is a permanent necessity, why not use it as a commentary on the absurdity of human arrangements which seem to reward a lucky few and to condemn others without a chance?

So we have an incongruous picture of a beggar who so behaves as to seem superior to the very people from whom he begs; it is they who must defend themselves for their actions and their high place in the world and to show cause why, in actual fact, the beggar is not more to be praised than the man who just happens to have the money.

Now the *schnorrer* arose from two facts in Jewish history and belief. There was a religious requirement that charity be given as part of one's service to God. Then too a persecuted and homeless people, wandering much in exile and often uprooted or disinherited by sudden visitations, produced many penniless and needy persons who had to get their living as best they could. Each wave of massacres turned up fresh hordes of the destitute. The two facts are of course allied. Because charity was so much needed, it became a religious requirement. From the beginning Jews had to fight adversity and there was always a need to help the unfortunate; as the *schnorrer* never ceases to point out, the *Torah* or Pentateuch expressly commands that help be given to the poor. Charity is a human duty since all men are equally of God; it is especially a Jewish obligation since philanthropy is demanded of those who have endured so much exile and oppression. Victims themselves they must never forget the sorrows of others, so that as a man and as a Jew one has to give. This compulsion cannot be overstressed; anyone who wants to obey God and be righteous *must* give charity.

Now, of course, such a high moral code is bound to encourage the cynical and the lazy who always exist and who see a chance to profit from society at no expense to themselves. It was easy for some *schnorrers* to abandon any pretense of work and simply to live off their communities. In the ghettos they could go from door to door and never be seen by gentiles, thus exploiting a religious and social privilege; they would not disgrace other Jews and would help them satisfy a religious duty. In earlier times the *schnorrer* might serve a useful purpose as a bearer of news. When his regular beat was confined he might, among other semi-useful activities, publish the day's obituary by going about the ghetto with a pyx, or money box; if one heard the rattle of this box one might ask the *schnorrer* who was dead today, and give him something for his information. Before the days of newspapers, the peripatetic *schnorrer* carried news about politics, discoveries, important developments of various kinds in business. Later he was the repository of anecdotes, humorous stories, and proverbial wit; indeed his name was derived from the Yiddish word for this kind of material.

But Zangwill's story is set in late 18th-century London under somewhat special conditions. There had been no Jewish community of any size in England after the expulsion under Edward I in 1290, and it was not until 1656 that the tiny group of Jews in London was openly accepted as within the law. In the course of time immigration to England from the continent became very cheap and easy; this encouraged the victims of any new persecutions to seek refuge where they would be unmolested.

Among hordes of abject and homeless fugitives, especially after the horrible Polish massacres in the mid-17th century, many were reduced to beggary and the number of *schnorrers* greatly increased. These were not only refugees from eastern Europe, but some who had fled the rigors of the Spanish inquisition, a more select and aristocratic group. The last of such large influxes came after the continental persecutions of 1768 when the English Jewish community more than doubled in size in thirty years. In time with the aid of the French revolutionary wars this large immigration stopped; the Jewish poor in London levelled off, and ceased to be a problem calling for the creation of a special class with its own name and function.

Now the great *schnorrer* whose exploits we are about to enjoy flourished at a time when a large pauper class had been imposed on the established Jews in London. Keep in mind that the oldest Jewish families were of Spanish-Portuguese origin called Sephardim, as distinguished from those of eastern Europe, the Ashkenazim or Tedescos. Our hero never lets anyone forget that he is a Sephardi, and it is worthwhile to emphasize that, along with their great antiquity and distinction in many other ways, the Sephardim were noted for generosity. Thus, the king of *schnorrers* finds himself at home in a charitable context. He is used to living with generous men, he is of their kind in birth and blood; he is therefore naturally placed toward charity which, as it happens, he receives instead of gives. He bears the proudest of all Sephardic names in addition, a name remarkable also for philanthropy. By birth, by association, by name he comes to his high expectation that charity will and should be bestowed upon him. His disdain of *schnorrers* with a mere Tedesco origin we will find among his most amusing traits as he proceeds on his parasitical way.

As a literary type, the *schnorrer* recalls one of the stock characters in, for example, Roman comedy where Peniculus (the Sponge) lives off the resources of others. As an example of Jewish humor the *schnorrer* arises from a tragic context of absolute human need to beg in order to live; from a consequent religious usage which enabled him to beg in order to create an opportunity of virtue in others; from, in turn, his own exploitation of the chance to live off a community, generous by custom and conviction; which finally persuades him that his way of life is entirely justified and indeed required for one so lofty and dignified, so learned and aristocratic as he.

Let us now make his acquaintance; he is presented by Israel Zangwill in a series of episodes which taken together become a minor classic of absurdity. The great philanthropist of London, Joseph Grobstock, is pleased one day to disburse from a large canvas bag a great many coins, each of which is separately wrapped in paper. Obviously well-known to a band of *schnorrers,* Grobstock is overwhelmed by customers for his bounty, each of whom receives one coin.

His bag still not empty, Grobstock comes upon a figure which could be nothing but that of a *schnorrer* but which has about it none the less something imposing and distinguished. The philanthropist reaches into the bag and offers one of the folded packets. Expecting some sign of gratitude, Grobstock is suddenly overwhelmed by a torrent of abuse. He has included one empty package in the whole sack, which it was his misfortune to bestow upon a man of regal deportment and a fierce sense of his own superiority in providing a chance for those who have money to display the virtue for the proper worship of God. Poor Grobstock does not escape from the encounter without paying a considerable sum for which he is thanked with dignity.

In answer to a question as to his name, the *schnorrer* gives this astounding reply: "I am Manasseh Bueno Barzillai Azevedo da Costa," a sonorous combination of some of the greatest of all Sephardic names. Poor Grobstock is reminded that Manasseh is indeed a Sephardi, even as it is written all over his own face that he is nothing but a Tedesco. He feels ever smaller and more inferior, as Manasseh establishes his towering intellect and aristocratic lineage above one who is clearly an upstart immigrant, a pitiful refugee from the ghettos of eastern Europe, whereas everyone knows the Sephardim have been in England for generations.

Grobstock can say or do nothing right as Manasseh maneuvers him into gifts of money and clothes, gets the better of him in an absurd contest as to who shall have the last good salmon in the fish-market, and loftily invites himself to have supper with Grobstock on the following Friday evening. To this supper he has the impudence to invite his friend Yankelé ben Yitzchok, and to speak with condescension of the food, while urging Yankelé to "make yourself at home—remember, you're my guest!"

Later Manasseh takes Yankelé to a play, which they behold from a box that has been entered over the protests of the attendant, largely on the strength of Manasseh's overpowering language and presence. It turns out that Yankelé, although an obvious Tedesco, aspires to the hand of Manasseh's daughter Deborah. The long argument as to whether Yankelé is able to support so high born a maiden properly, whether the sources of his income as a *schnorrer* are contaminated by anything that might be called work, whether he is able to give a suitable example of his powers as a *schnorrer* so as to insure a regular income, and what the terms of Deborah's own dowry should be—these emerge in a dialogue preposterous in the last degree.

When the marriage is agreed upon, Manasseh finds himself censured by the Mahamad, the all-powerful governing body of the Sephardic congregation, which is naturally opposed to a union between Ashkenazim and Sephardim. Once more Manasseh triumphs by a display of superior learning and ingenious self-justification, but demonstrates his real greatness and royal stature in his declaration of gifts to the synagogue. These he announces publicly before the congregation, electrifying the entire body by listing gifts to the absolutely unheard of amount of a hundred pounds. As he has not a cent of this money available, he is obliged to go out and collect it. The process of collection shows Manasseh's genius in all of its elements, until at last he maneuvers poor Grobstock once more into assisting him. The philanthropist is about to make a killing of his own through shrewd investments, and manages to increase the money Manasseh has collected tenfold, so that the great man is not only able to pay the hundred pounds he has pledged, but also to create a charitable fund of five hundred pounds whose income he generously stipulates shall be given by the Mahamad to a poor and deserving member of the congregation. The donor is of course to decide who shall receive the annuity. The Mahamad eagerly accepts these conditions, whereupon the donor's choice falls upon Manasseh Bueno Barzillai Azevedo da Costa, who goes down in history forever after as *The King of Schnorrers.*

Zangwill has been content to assemble these episodes around three main contests: Manasseh against Grobstock, against Yankelé, and against the Sephardic authorities. In each case what seems to be inferior actually wins out over something higher and greater than itself. As Manasseh outwits and overwhelms both Grobstock and the Mahamad who are vastly above him in society, so in turn Yankelé prevails over a far mightier man than he. But Manasseh wins out by arrogance and a display of force from his natural superiority, while Yankelé prevails by flattery and insinuation and pretending to seem inferior.

This theme of incongruous victory unifies the story at one level and gives the episodes more continuity than the overall action calls for. Much of the humor recalls Joseph Wechsberg's *New Yorker* sketch of the great Joseph Schostal, leader of the all-powerful claque at the Vienna Opera. Here too a serious profession is made out of a piece of absurd quackery, and we are entertained by ludicrous deception and vanity in a world which seems to make no sense or to pretend to justice anyway. We end with the cynical assumption that all activities are not really what they seem to be, that they are based on some form of cheating, until outright fraud becomes defensible as being only a question of degree.

But the materials before us are much too funny to depress us by their sadder implications. They center largely upon Manasseh, of course, who is a loose combination of aristocracy, intellect, and religion. In varying degrees he entertains us by displays of arrogance, shrewdness, parasitism, vanity, and ingenious self-justification. Most of these qualities emerge at the outset when we hear his name: Manasseh Bueno Barzillai Azevedo da Costa, an original literary construction of his own, we are sure.

The mellifluous words sound the note of incongruity for Manasseh throughout. We see the ludicrous contrast between what he is and what his name implies: all that Manasseh is not in the eyes of the world. Certainly these elaborate and euphonious words contrast sharply with the harsh consonants of Joseph Grobstock. This is solid and crude, a piece of common wood, like the uncultivated homeliness of what the man does for a living. The word Grobstock says directly what he is about and is done with it. Da Costa the aristocrat is not about anything and can take all the time necessary to say what his name is.

This becomes an end in itself, not a convenient label for someone bent on productive work. The words da Costa call for our hero's manner and bearing, his aristocratic assurance. The flowing vowels and liquid tone of the full name roll out sonorously; all but one of the five units contain long vowels, whereas Grobstock has only two names with but one long vowel buried amid a thicket of encumbering consonants.

A glamorous, romantic Spaniard of remote and ancient origins makes pitiful the homely German Grobstock, vulgarized by trade and the coarse associations of the market-place which have never besmirched the aristocratic culture of da Costa. The very length of this name implies ease and leisure—not the hurried, bare functionalism and practicality of Joseph Grobstock. Its complexity suggests also the noble or royal figures who have to include a series of various units in what they are called so as to take into account their complicated origins, branches, and ancestral obligations. The preposition "da" carries similar hints of being of or from an ancient place, whereas again a meagre single name like Grobstock seems to come from an occupation of some kind like miller, smith, or clerk. If one's name describes the work one does, or implies work of any kind, all is revealed and there is no concealing a plebeian origin. Da Costa therefore allows nothing to suggest that work was ever done or should be done; this becomes central to his own professional outlook. It all breathes an air of command, of privilege, of high expectation, of taking for granted the homage, the labor, and tribute of lesser men.

The names of the two antagonists then are keys to their worlds. Da Costa is a hellenist, a child of light and ideas; Grobstock has little discernment, taste, or delicacy, no metaphysical adroitness able to make remote connections, no skill to phrase them until they seem inevitable. A routine fellow without ideas, he has only wealth, respectability, and worldly success to compensate for his dullness. And who would have these at the price of being so devoid of taste and fluency? Not

Manasseh Bueno Barzillai Azevedo da Costa certainly. This superbly constructed name is borne by a professional beggar, and creates a delightfully comic incongruity.

Manasseh's appearance goes not with his name, however, but with his profession, and thus appearance leads directly to a most amusing episode when poor Grobstock hopes to change it for the better by the offer of some clothes.

When he first saw Manasseh, Grobstock beheld the unmistakable *schnorrer*. The tall figure was wearing a home-made turban, assembled out of a black cap and white handkerchief. His waistcoat had its first nine buttons open, and a heavy over-garment like a blanket "with buttons the size of compasses and flaps reaching nearly to his shoe buckles" hung down over an undercoat which already reached the bottoms of his knee-breeches. The overcoat was worn clockwise with dangling sleeves, and the general effect of this shabby, snuff-colored outfit was one of picturesque dilapidation. The accompanying personality had an air of aristocratic dignity in spite of a generally unwashed and unshaven state. A jet-black beard ran up to meet equally dark hair, framing a vivid face in black. "It was a long, tapering face with sanguine lips gleaming at the heart of a black bush; the eyes were large and lambent, set in deep sockets under black arching eyebrows; the nose was long and coptic; the brow low but broad, with straggling wisps of hair protruding from beneath the turban. His right hand grasped a plain ashen staff."

Manasseh so overwhelms Grobstock that he is incapable of defending himself from the beggar's condescension.

"Do you know what I have a mind to do? To come

and be your Sabbath-guest! Yes, I will take supper with you next Friday. . . . Never before have I sat at the table of a Tedesco—but you—you are a man after my own heart. . . . Next Friday at six—do not forget."

Fleeced of his money by numerous ingenuities, Grobstock is finally so far behind in the verbal duel that he has forgotten his grievances; then Manasseh invites himself to supper with the air of a man patronizing a social inferior. His victim is terrified to refuse. Yet it is unthinkable that he admit such a scarecrow to his table, especially in view of his liveried servant Wilkinson. He, also, makes Grobstock feel inferior and might humiliate his master by the attitude he would undoubtedly assume toward Manasseh.

Grobstock gets the happy idea then of offering some of his clothes to the *schnorrer,* who is after all a fine figure of a man, and if well-dressed might be passed off as a foreign prince and so become acceptable to the disdainful Wilkinson. But Manasseh agrees to accept the clothes only after some hesitation on professional grounds. It must be clear that no one else has a right to expect the clothes, that there is no official clothes-receiver attached to Grobstock, and so "on condition that I am to have the appointment permanently, of course," Manasseh loftily consents to take the clothes.

But poor Grobstock is worse off than ever; Manasseh insists on removing the garments immediately, so that Wilkinson is bound to see him in all of his unclean disarray. Besides, Manasseh anticipates future gifts of clothing and acts as if the very garments his benefactor is now wearing were his own. Grobstock wishes to sustain his composure by taking a good pinch of snuff, but Manasseh cries to him imperiously to stand still. It seems that snuff has been spilled on the coat front and

Manasseh insists on brushing it off to the last particle. When Grobstock mutters "that will do," he is told that it will not do.

"I cannot have my coat spoiled. By the time it comes to me it will be a mass of stains if I don't look after it."

"Oh, is that why you took so much trouble?" said Grobstock, with an easy laugh.

"Why else? Do you take me for a beadle, a brusher of gaiters? . . . . There now, that is the cleanest I can get it. You would escape the droppings if you held your snuff-box so—" Manasseh gently took the snuff-box and began to explain.

Later on at the dreadful supper, Manasseh is concerned for what his host is wearing. "Take care," he cries anxiously to Grobstock at his own table. "You are spluttering sauce all over that waistcoat, without any consideration for me." Thus lessons in manners and deportment are combined with proper care for Manasseh's own property and his professional dignity as official clothes-receiver to Grobstock.

Meanwhile, however, the clothes must be actually received at Grobstock's house and this encounter enables Manasseh to display again his typical methods and their accompanying absurdities. The question arises as to whether Grobstock has left anything in the pockets. The poor man stammers an apologetic, "Do you—do you—mind my looking?" and is as usual overwhelmed by the reply: "Am I a dog? . . . . Am I a thief that you should go over my pockets? If, when I get home . . . I find anything in my pockets that is of no value to anybody but you, do you fear I will not return it? If, on the other hand, I find anything that is of value to me, do you fear I will not keep it?"

Even though the befuddled Grobstock can see vaguely

that Manasseh is begging the question—"professionally enough" as Zangwill interpolates—he is able to mutter only a feeble "No, but—but. . . ." This gives Manasseh an opening for another favorite device, the appeal to Scripture. False logic, religious precedent, and learning are all employed.

"But what? . . . Surely you need not me to teach you your duty. You cannot be ignorant of the Law of Moses on the point." Inasmuch as Manasseh's vocation is of a semi-religious nature anyway, he seems to feel himself almost a member of the clergy and has an appropriate familiarity with the clerical materials of admonition. The pedestrian Grobstock declares that the Law of Moses had said nothing about money found in the pockets of clothing given to the poor. This shows that he has no capacity to read the Law for its full implications. So he is again defeated:

> Indeed! What says Deuteronomy? "When thou reapest thine harvest in thy field, and hast forgot a sheaf in the field, thou shalt not go again to fetch it: it shall be for the stranger, for the fatherless, and for the widow." Is it not further forbidden to go over the boughs of thy olive-tree again, or to gather the fallen fruit of thy vineyard? You will admit that Moses would have added a prohibition against searching minutely the pockets of cast-off garments, were it not that for forty years our ancestors had to wander in the wilderness in the same clothes, which miraculously waxed with their growth.

Having thus left Grobstock far behind once more, Manasseh soothes him with an air of judicious fairness, as he has observed other evidence that the philanthropist is a devout adherent of the law. Mollified and relieved at last, Grobstock agrees to let the clothes go as they are. Just as he imagines that his troubles will end Manasseh utters a cry of outraged injury. Three times, until his voice is rising to a shriek, Manasseh tells Grobstock, "I miss a pair of pantaloons." From the original pile of clothes agreed upon, one pair has been removed when Manasseh is out of the room. The poor owner finally stammers something about a new pair which has accidentally been mixed up with the older garments. Here Manasseh's appeal is to the language of chivalry, of the aristocrat and the gentleman, as well as to ordinary decency toward the helpless poor:

"Of course I mean the new pair! And so you took them away! Just because I wasn't looking. I left the room, thinking I had to do with a man of honour. If you had taken an old pair I shouldn't have minded so much; but to rob a poor man of his brand-new breeches!"

He gives up the pantaloons, but even in temporary defeat Manasseh keeps an air of "sorrowful *hauteur*" which puts Grobstock in his place as the mean-spirited clodhopper that he is. The beggar's final triumph chills the blood of his benefactor. Manasseh appears for Friday supper looking exactly as before. His costume has not changed in the least; he has merely sold the clothes to a dealer, pocketed the money, and compounded Grobstock's humiliation by bringing unannounced the unspeakable Yankele as a guest, a clumsy, dumpy figure, even dingier than himself, "with a cajoling grin on his mud-coloured, hairy face. Neither removed his headgear."

These first encounters with Grobstock show how inseparable one from the other the three main lines of Manasseh's character are. His aristocracy, learning and intellect, and religious devotion are all involved one with another; in the end we will find that they cannot be separated from his beggary. A man of such overwhelming perfections cannot take a place among ordinary men in the world, and he persuades us that he has no choice but to beg from a society controlled by people so vastly inferior to him.

Manasseh's aristocracy had asserted itself immediately against Grobstock who admitted that he was a Tedesco, although he was proud of being a financier, an East India director, and rich as any Sephardi. Manasseh's reply was a mingling of social snobbery, of religious and hereditary self-righteousness based on a knowledge of history and the great Jewish past:

> Your community is yet young and struggling—your rich men are as the good men in Sodom for multitude. You are the immigrants of yesterday—refugees from the Ghettos of Russia and Poland and Germany. But we, as you are aware, have been established here for generations; in the Peninsula our ancestors graced the courts of kings, and controlled the pursestrings of princes; in Holland we held the empery of trade. Ours have been the poets and scholars in Israel. You cannot expect that we should recognize your rabble, which prejudices us in the eyes of England. We made the name of Jew honourable; you degrade it. You are as the mixed multitude which came up with our forefathers out of Egypt.

Historically Manasseh might have a point here, even though it could be more appropriately made by someone other than a beggar from the view of those who would think themselves examples of the superiority he is maintaining. It is certainly true that east European Jews were far more common in England by Manasseh's time, more numerous, later in arriving, and far more of a problem than the smaller group of Sephardic Jews of long standing. In 1657 almost all of the some thirty-five families in London were Sephardim; by 1800, of some 20,000 Jews, only one-fifth were Sephardim. Manasseh may well assert that he is one of a very special and exclusive caste, because the great old families were diminishing as newcomers from eastern Europe poured in.

Manasseh's high birth would show in his dignified bearing and imperious manner, even if he said nothing of his actual origin. The austere Wilkinson himself was permitted to doubt the beggar's status. After all, Manasseh might be an eccentric whose conceit it was to go about defying convention in his outlandish getup. Grobstock was made to wonder; perhaps it was all a joke, a prank.

"Did not a natural aristocracy ooze from every pore of his mysterious visitor? Was not every tone, every gesture, that of a man born to rule?" Even Mme. Grobstock, a woman who had "a permanent air of remembering the exact figure of her dowry," was impressed by the *schnorrer's* familiarity with ancient usage. Manasseh appealed to "beautiful custom" in referring to his being a "Sabbath guest." In anyone else this would seem like what it was—an inexcusably rude and insensitive intrusion on personal privacy; it seemed acceptable now because Manasseh's air of assurance implied a custom honored from of old among the ancient Spanish grandees, from whom he did not blush to descend.

His final triumph over Grobstock touches upon the

one unthinkable condescension for an aristocrat—marriage beneath his station. Manasseh piously hopes that the Lord will bless his hostess with many children, saying, "I should be pleased to marry your daughter if you had one."

Grobstock himself of course misunderstands this, and cries, "You marry my daughter!"

The reply is grandly absurd: "Who else moves among better circles—would be more easily able to find her a suitable match?"

More calmly Grobstock murmurs, "Oh, in that sense . . ."

"In what other sense? You do not think that I, a Sephardi, would marry her myself!"

Manasseh sees no contradiction between his aristocratic lineage and his work, if it can be called that, as a marriage broker. His lineage would, however, be grossly offended by his making an unsuitable marriage with the daughter of a rich Tedesco. Being marriage broker is all right for a *schnorrer,* and of course there is no contradiction between aristocracy of birth and *schnorring,* on the contrary. Yankelé seems not to grasp these refinements since he aspires to marry Manasseh's own daughter.

When they have finally left the Grobstocks in peace Yankelé ventures to suggest that Manasseh might have married a daughter of their recent host. But there cannot be any compromise here: "Guard your tongue! A Sephardi cannot marry a Tedesco. It would be a degradation."

But the real mark of Manasseh's high birth is one which shows that *schnorring* and aristocracy are one. This is established in a dialogue of fabulous absurdity on the question of work, and the absolute necessity which forbids a *schnorrer* to betray his profession by working in any form. He must not work, any more than he must do any of the other things by which people seem to become rich and successful. Just as he is outraged by Yankelé's assumption that he might pay for theatre tickets—"Did you think I was going to pay?" he gasped—so Manasseh regards work as distinctly beneath him. It is not only unbecoming for an aristocrat, an intellectual, and a student of the *Talmud* to work like lesser men; experience shows that work is an uncertain, insecure way of making a living. As the preposterous dialogue unfolds, one wonders at the amount of energy and ingenious calculation spent in avoiding work, until it would seem easier just to be an honest laborer.

Not so Manasseh. Yankelé says that he is professionally so successful he can easily support the great man's daughter out of his earnings as *schnorrer*. He lists one after another the sources of his income and Manasseh reviews them to make sure that no work whatsoever is involved. It is a matter of principle, of professional conviction and dignity on the highest level:

> Surely you know that *schnorring* and work should never be mixed. A man cannot do two things properly. He must choose his profession and stick to it. A friend of mine once succumbed to the advice of the philanthropists instead of asking mine. He had one of the best provincial rounds in the kingdom, but in every town he weakly listened to the lectures of the president of the congregation inculcating work, and at last he actually invested the savings of years in jewelry, and went round trying to peddle it. The presidents . . . all expressed their pleasure at his working for a living, and showing a

> manly independence. "But I *schnorr* also," he reminds them, holding out his hand. . . . It was in vain. No one gave him a farthing. He had blundered beyond redemption. At one blow he had destroyed one of the most profitable connections a *Schnorrer* ever had, and without even getting anything for the goodwill. . . . A *Schnorrer* cannot be too careful. And once you begin to work, where are you to draw the line?

The incongruity is compounded by the language of formal business and professional life, the very life which the *schnorrer's* refusal to work so completely repudiates. Manasseh's rhetoric is always magnificent and in the complex dialogue he delivers some fine strokes by use of one of his favorite devices, the question or the indignant, incredulous outcry to which there can be only one answer. Among the sources of his income, Yankelé boasts that he makes ten guineas a year by synagogue-knocking.

> "Stop a minute! I cannot pass that item! . . . Synagogue-knocking is distinctly work. . . . if going round early in the morning to knock at the doors of twenty pious persons, and rouse them for morning service isn't work, then the Christian bell-ringer is a beggar. No, no! Profits from this source I cannot regard as legitimate. . . . I call it debasing. What! To assist at the services for a fee! To worship one's Maker for hire! Under such conditions to pray is to work!" His breast swelled with majesty and scorn.

But there is an even worse objection. Enough that work is despicable, illegitimate, treasonous to a high aristocratic ideal; it does not even repay the ignominy of engaging in it. On its own terms work is contemptible. Manasseh will not give his daughter to anyone who works and certainly not to a *schnorrer* who makes illegitimate profits. You get money today, but what about tomorrow? "Work of whatever kind is by its very nature unreliable. At any moment trade may be slack." And if your trade relies on the piety of others, you are in danger of losing money because people may at any moment become less pious! Thus with an almost Swiftian subtlety the language of standard occupations is used to decry them, and the most uncertain of incomes pretends to question as unstable what alone is supposed to guarantee security.

The references to piety, however, do not prevent Manasseh from asserting a further paradox. Even though people may become less devout and so give less money for synagogue-knocking and the like, still *schnorring* is the surest livelihood because of its religious sanction. This doctrine is central to Manasseh's character and way of life; it is an ingenious compound of business calculation, paternal feeling, and religious authority:

> *Schnorring* is the only occupation that is regular all the year around. . . . Everything else may fail—the greatest commercial houses may totter to the ground; as it is written, "He humbleth the proud." But the *Schnorrer* is always secure. Whoever falls, there are always enough left to look after *him*. If you were a father, Yankelé, you would understand my feelings. How can a man allow his daughter's future happiness to repose on a basis so uncertain as work? No, no.

Finally Manasseh defends *schnorring* on human grounds, condemns the modern movement toward organized charity which has in recent times ended the existence of his kind, and justifies *schnorring* for its religious benefit to others.

> I always held strongly that the rich should be visited in their own homes, and I grieve to see this personal touch, this contact with the very people to whom you give the good deeds, being replaced by lifeless circulars. One owes it to one's position in life to afford the wealthy classes the opportunity of charity warm from the heart; they should not be neglected and driven in their turn to write cheques in cold blood, losing all that human sympathy which comes from personal intercourse—as it is written, "Charity delivers from death."

Miraculously the private charity which is so much more profitable to the *schnorrer* turns out also to have a greater spiritual value for its donor. Can one say that charity which is given through a secretary and published in annual reports "has so great a redeeming power as that slipped privately into the hands of the poor man, who makes a point of keeping secret from every donor what he has received from the others?" Manasseh is so carried away by his rhetoric that he misses Yankelé's dry sarcasm, "I am glad you don't call collecting de money vork."

At times this religious sanction is supported by such heavy Biblical allusion that Manasseh seems like one of the prophets or judges, a voice sent from God for the stern admonition of the unholy. And the *Talmud* enjoins relief and aid to the poor by charitable deeds as much as by learning and study. It is full of proverbs, maxims, and concentrated wisdom upon which Manasseh constantly draws, so as to seem unanswerably right before anyone else can think of what to say. The *Talmud* asserts that charity is the most important element in the worship of God, so Manasseh can justify himself at will on the highest authority.

The plodding Grobstock cannot match this fluent and ready justification for what would otherwise seem outlandish. When Manasseh receives the empty packet his misfortune is turned against one who has mocked the misery of the poor. "The Holy One, blessed be He, has punished you for your heartless jesting with the poor." Grobstock is "making a sport for yourself of their misfortunes, even as the Philistines sported with Samson." God has taken from the magnate the good deed which might have been put to his account. "He has declared you unworthy of achieving righteousness through me. Go your way, murderer!"

This seems like a harsh view of his action to Grobstock, but again Grobstock has not read the *Talmud* carefully enough. "Yes, Murderer. Stands it not in the *Talmud* that he who shames another is as one who spills his blood? And have you not put me to shame?"

And this is by no means all:

> Epicurean! . . . Blasphemer! Is it thus you would palter with the sacred texts? Do you forget what the next verse says:—Bloodthirsty and deceitful men shall not live out half their days—? Shame on you. . . . Has not the beadle of your Synagogue boasted to me that you have given him a guinea for brushing your spatterdashes? Would you think of offering him a packet? Nay, it is the poor that are trodden on—they whose merits are in excess of those of beadles. But the Lord will find others to take up his

> loans—for he who hath pity on the poor lendeth to the Lord. You are no true son of Israel.

If only Grobstock had as refined a sense of his duty as Manasseh has of the poor man's obligation! He knows that he must make it easier for Grobstock to shower benefits on him and is willing to carry out this duty and perform a great favor thereby. Grobstock only seems unaware of the *Talmud* which has called charity the salt of riches. He is afflicted by conventional notions of high and low, of who plays the superior role in this life. Let him consider the truth of this classical statement and his soul will be saved:

> Hush! The world could not exist without *Schnorrers*. As it is written, "And Repentance and Prayer and CHARITY avert the evil decree." Charity is put last—it is the climax—the greatest thing on earth. And the *Schnorrer* is the greatest man on earth; for it stands in the *Talmud*. "He who causes is greater than he who does." Therefore, the *Schnorrer* who causes charity is even greater than he who gives it.

Manasseh's Learning and Triumph

Now Manasseh's generosity in providing an outlet for charity has another sanction. Not only is he poor, he is also learned. He can thus profit both from the Jewish law of charity and from a respect for intellect as well. In the days when the Jewish community had public-relief funds, certain priorities were established. Relief to the scholar was held superior to charity for one who was ignorant, so that Manasseh could demand support on the ground of his scholarship alone. His acceptance of the Jewish reverence for learning could even go so far that he might forget the superiority of Sephardim over Ashkenazim.

The doltish Grobstock praises the great prize fighter Dan Mendoza, but Manasseh disdains such a coarse fellow. "I would willingly exchange our Dan Mendoza for your David Levi," he says; actually David Levi's only claim to notice is a literary one. He is "the literary ornament of the Ghetto; a shoe-maker and hat-dresser who cultivated Hebrew philosophy and the Muses," and defends his creed against Priestley and Paine. There is simply no escaping the traditional Jewish demand for a well-stored mind, as Yankelé is reminded. The dictum of the sages is quite clear: " 'To give your daughter to an uncultured man is like throwing her bound to a lion.' "

As Manasseh says of himself, "I am a son of the law, a student of the *Talmud.*"

His grasp of the Jewish intellectual inheritance becomes one of his strongest weapons in the constant fight he wages to establish his superiority over other men and hence his right to beg from them. For clearly Manasseh must be superior in mind and attainment, not through being rich and powerful. He must be superior in the only way one can be without external means. His scholarship must therefore be impeccable if Manasseh is to meet his own terms. In the Jewish world which he inhabits, the scholar is honored as being and possessing on a high level what everyone would want or would get as his own if he could. The scholar is and has what everyone wants to be and have; hence it is that people like Grobstock who are and have only tangible and material things must recognize Manasseh's real superiority, must suspect that after all he may be right to patronize them. For he has studied the *Torah* and the *Talmud;* he knows the *law,* as he is constantly pointing out, and indeed must know it if he is to seem higher than other men and rightly to demand their deference and charity for his learning as well as for his poverty.

The Jews were much concerned for their own law after the breakup of their state in 70 A.D. A separate group with no political entity, at the mercy of whatever lords they happened to live under, forbidden to assimilate with their neighbors or masters—they naturally had to make their own rules, had to study and keep them with precision. This was all they had of their own to unify and sustain them.

The great storehouse of Jewish law and ethical teaching is in the *Torah,* meaning doctrine, and embracing the five books of the Pentateuch. This is the most sacred of Jewish inheritances, the ultimate statement of divine revelation, the everlasting word; the study of this imperishable wisdom is therefore the highest ideal of human activity. The Jewish intellectual tradition and respect for learning are based on this ideal study, an activity transcending any other and outweighing in value even the rescue of a human life, or the honor of one's parents. Manasseh must show familiarity with the law, then, or he cannot pretend to be superior to other Jews.

The *Talmud* relies heavily on the *Torah,* cites and praises it at every turn. A body of commentary and interpretation of Jewish law accumulated by rabbis and other scholars over the centuries, the *Talmud* devotes a vast amount of space to legal distinctions and admonitions, to the need for study and acquiring knowledge in the most uncompromising sense. Manasseh's learning then shows that he is indeed what he should be. A Jew should be studious in order to understand his inheritance, especially his religion; hence Zangwill ingeniously makes Manasseh's mental equipment inseparable from his religion, and both are naturally related to his *schnorring.* The word *Talmud* means learning and study, the book itself suggesting by its very bulk and complexity what a proper Jew must know if he is to do justice to his inheritance. A gigantic accumulation in thousands of pages, the *Talmud* is the product of centuries of life and thought, a whole library in itself. Manasseh exhibits a prodigious familiarity with it, and uses its high authority to silence at once the unworthy antagonists who are incapable of using its riches.

Manasseh puts the august Mahamad itself out of countenance by his superior knowledge of the law, not only of the traditional Talmudic variety, but of the ancient Ascamot, the Sephardic rule which the Mahamad exists to sustain and interpret. Summoned before this "arbitrary and inquisitorial" council of five, Manasseh has the audacity to keep them waiting and turns all their efforts to reprove him back upon themselves. They are, among other things, offended by his making no move to take off his filthy headgear in their presence. The Chancellor angrily implies that if Manasseh were a gentleman "you would take that thing off your head." Manasseh replies that, "If you were not a Man-of-the Earth . . . you would know that it is not a mark of disrespect for the Mahamad, but of respect for the Law, which is higher than the Mahamad. The rich man can afford to neglect our holy religion, but the poor man has only the Law. It is his sole luxury."

Manasseh now proceeds to expose the ignorance of the very custodians of Sephardic law by showing that there is nothing in the sacred Ascamot to forbid the marriage of his daughter with Yankelé. The original Ascamot or constitution was drawn up in 1663 when the first Mahamad of the English Jewish community was established. The original body of rule contained forty-two laws, including the one simple and absolute declaration that "the Mahamad shall have authority and supremacy over everything."

But the Mahamad of Manasseh's time probably lacked one essential which would never be neglected by so superb an intellectual aristocrat as Manasseh: Manasseh knew Portuguese better than they did. Manasseh stood for the values of the past regardless of the movement of time which so often leaves behind the original beauty and power of an institution. By now, Portuguese had been a dead letter to most English Sephardim; yet all announcements in the synagogue and all records of the community were made in Portuguese. Until 1819 the minutes of the Mahamad were kept in Portuguese and the Ascamot were not translated into English until then. The Mahamad should have known Portuguese well, but English was steadily creeping into the discussion; so long of course as the Ascamot were in Portuguese their authority would be greatly enhanced, and Manasseh took full advantage of this fact.

After magnificently declaiming, Manasseh announces that there is no ancient Ascama which has anything to say against a Sephardi marrying a Tedesco. "It was as though he had disavowed the Decalogue." The answer is that "It has never been legislated against, because it has never been conceived possible. These things are an instinct with every right-minded Sephardi." The councillor thinks by this assertion to confound Manasseh, and follows it by the question, "Have we ever legislated against marrying Christians?" The poor man is overwhelmed. "Certainly, we have," Manasseh announces.

> "In Section XX, Paragraph II." He quoted the Ascama by heart, rolling out the sonorous Portuguese like a solemn indictment. "If our legislators had intended to prohibit intermarriage with the German community, they would have prohibited it."

So there is no Ascama prohibiting the admission of Yankelé to full privileges. Actually Manasseh has come before the Mahamad only to ask that his son-in-law might "receive the bridegroom's call to the Law on the Sabbath before his marriage. . . . By Section III, Paragraph I, you are empowered to admit any person about to marry the daughter of a Yahid." Once more

Manasseh intones the magnificent cadences of the original Portuguese, every syllable an indictment of the councillors for their ignorance, their own failure to live up to what their office calls for. In spite of this exposure by a beggar, the councillors are thrilled by the "quintessential awfulness of ancient statutes in a tongue not understood."

But the Chancellor is the one antagonist who knows the law as well as Manasseh and he now thinks to play his hand at its strongest. He points out that in fact Manasseh is not a Yahid, a member of the congregation, because anyone whose name appears on the charity list ceases to be a regular member. But this only invites Manasseh's standard defense of his calling, the ingenious combination of piety and question-begging self-justification. After all, who keeps the community together if it is not those who take charity, if it is not those who provide an outlet for the fines that are constantly levied by the Mahamad? The *schnorrer* once more becomes indispensable, a necessity to those from whom he begs.

The absurdity of the humor here recalls the great classical scene in the Marx brothers' *Animal Crackers*. A picture has been stolen, no one knows by whom. Perhaps it was taken by the man in the house next door? But there is no house next door, so there can't be a man in it who might have stolen the picture. In that case, we must build a house next door in order to provide a place for the man to live, who if he lived there or if there were a house for him to live in, might have been the one who stole the picture. And so on into a discussion so preposterous one can hardly bear to laugh any longer.

So with this defense of *schnorring*. A Jew has to give

alms, and in order to give them he needs a recipient. He can't give charity unless there are some poor people to take it, and if no one is poor, then someone has to act as a poor man so that the chance to show the virtue of alms-giving will be provided for those of whom it is required. The *schnorrer* becomes a religious and public benefactor deserving of honor in the community.

When at last Manasseh's impudence and slippery ingenuity have defeated the Mahamad, the meeting breaks up with the president falling in an apoplectic faint. As the wretched man lies there breathing heavily and everyone is in a panic, Manasseh alone is composed and able to draw upon his learning and piety as always. A sly reference to his Portuguese origin reminds the councillors of his superiority over them once more:

> "You see, gentlemen, how insecure is earthly power," said the *Schnorrer* solemnly, while the President breathed stertorously, deaf to his impressive moralising. "It is swallowed up in an instant, as Lisbon was engulfed. Cursed are they who despise the poor. How is the saying of our sages verified—The house that opens not to the poor opens to the physician—" His eyes shone with unearthly radiance in the gathering gloom.
>
> The cowed assembly wavered before his words, like reeds before the wind, or conscience-stricken kings before fearless prophets.

Manasseh's intellect is impressive for what is stored there, its immense freight of apt quotation and allusion to ancient documents, his ready command of the accumulated wisdom and religious principle of the Jewish race. Manasseh is of course extremely Jewish, belligerently so at all times, but nowhere more amusingly than in his feeling for extreme refinements of meaning, for nice distinctions of title and function, and for the triumph of acuteness of mind over the actual fact in a given situation. Obviously other people have gone in for similar hair-splitting, so that this aspect of Manasseh's comedy is not Jewish by definition. None the less it was encouraged by Jewish history and practice, and comes through here as one of the most amusing sides of a wildly ludicrous character.

More comic situations will develop in a society that calls for a vast multiplication of function and title. Certainly the Jewish religion and a self-contained life driven back on itself called for endless ceremonies and functions, with requirements to be minutely learned and observed, all important to the whole and demanding special performance by special individuals.

Sholom Aleichem makes this highly amusing in a story of the festival of Purim when custom demanded the mutual delivery of sweetmeats to all the people one was related to or friendly with. The offerings had to be carried out with precision as to weight, number and materials used. A great minuteness and delicacy of observance, of recollection, a sense of value and distinction, of absolute propriety and correctness of usage had to be observed. One had to know exactly how much and what was called for by whom, from whom and to whom. The exact practices of other years had to be respected and every distinction of office, class, personal honor or social status, had to be recalled so that the rich, the poor, the rabbi, the synagogue trustees, the cantor, the ritual slaughterer, and everyone else got the precise offering that was his due.

Such refinement naturally leads to the many jokes having to do with insulted personal vanity and dignity.

This is the other side of jokes, also very numerous and amusing, which arise from people's not being what they are supposed to be or what they profess to be. The more different things people are supposed to be or do, the more chance there is for absurdity in not living up to what is called for.

The Jewish community was heavily specialized and compartmentalized into offices, duties, posts, and kinds of activity or obligation involving ceremonial or professional knowledge which made for a variety of pretense and deception on the one hand, as well as injured vanity and professional jealousy on the other. The marriage-broker, the *schnorrer,* the mourner, the funeral preacher, the grave-watcher, the bell-ringer, the ritual slaughterer, the circumcision expert, and many others gave a chance for the comedy of offended personal dignity, of invaded prerogative and jealously guarded precedence.

Such minute subdivisions, with everyone entitled to certain things that go with his special place and function, have to be known and observed minutely or dire offense will be given. So with a perfectly straight face a sense of outrage will be registered over nothing at all, an incongruous tempest over nothing emerges in a closely organized life. This will be true in a small, self-contained group that has only its own relationships and values to consume life. People have to concern themselves with what there is in the group itself, and they have to achieve an enormous variety in a little space when the variety of life as a whole is denied them.

Now Manasseh is acutely sensitive and loves refined distinctions of all kinds. Any form of ancient practice or ritual, any prerogative a knowledge of which will display his piety and learning, is especially welcome to him. He constantly quotes or refers to such niceties to shame and confound his antagonists. This is at once the result of conditions imposed on Jewish life, and of certain qualities of the mind which are naturally developed.

The first of these is carried to its most absurd length when the debate on Yankelé's candidacy for Deborah's hand is in progress. It seems that each has to keep in mind that the other is divided into a number of persons, corresponding to the various services that have to be paid for. When Yankelé says that he can support Deborah, Manasseh reminds him that he has formerly pretended to be very poor. The answer is that Yankelé says he is poor when speaking as a *schnorrer,* but "As a suitor I tell you I can *schnorr* enough to keep two vives."

Manasseh demands to know in return, "Do you tell this to da Costa the father or da Costa the marriage-broker?"

In turn, part of Yankelé's income depends on a certain number of free meals, some of which he will expect to get from Manasseh as his father-in-law, who will in turn be less inclined to give these meals if he knows that Yankelé is very well off and doesn't really need them. The answer to this divides Manasseh into four parts since as he is told, "You are too much a man of honour to know as a private philanthropist vat I have told de marriage-broker, de fader-in-law and de fellow *Schnorrer*. Besides, I would have de free meals from you as de son-in-law, not de *Schnorrer*."

But the defense of Yankelé's ability to support Deborah turns upon showing that his various activities bring in a total of one hundred-fifty pounds a year. Here the remarkable quickness as well as retentiveness of

Manasseh's mind astounds his future son-in-law, when at the end of his minute and complicated recital Manasseh informs him that including everything mentioned, even items that are not entirely legitimate, his total income amounts to only one hundred forty-three pounds nineteen shillings. Yankelé is simply staggered and demands to know how Manasseh can be so exact. All the while the great man has been memorizing each item and now replies sternly as follows:

"Do you think I cannot do simple addition? . . . Are not these your ten items?

Synagogue Pension, with Passover extras ...	8	0	0
Synagogue-knocking	10	10	0
District Visiting	65	0	0
As Congregation-man and Pyx-bearer	14	0	0
Year-Times	15	0	0
Palm-branch and Trumpet Fees	6	6	0
Purim-presents, etc.	3	3	0
Sale of Clothes	4	10	0
Equivalent of Free Meals	7	0	0
Miscellanea, the unexpected	10	10	0
Total ...	143	19	0"

The incongruous linking of religion and business here is only a shade less ridiculous than the counting-house atmosphere surrounding the dowry and the negotiations for the fortune that will of course accompany a genuine princess. Zangwill has elsewhere in *Rose of the Ghetto* developed the comedy of the so-called marriage-broker, whose stock-market title underlines the inherent absurdity of his calling. The broker uses a ridiculously cynical and realistic terminology in trying to persuade others into an action which is supposed to be based on romantic and idealized love. Now Manasseh is acting as marriage-broker for his own daughter, and while promising a dowry "befitting her station" as he says, he feels some reluctance to have her marry anything less than a king of *schnorrers.* Yankelé promises that he will indeed be such a king since if he gets Deborah he will have *schnorred* the most precious thing there is from one who is himself a king, and above all, "I shall have *schnorred* your services as marriage-broker into de bargain."

Yankelé is to show his mettle in a final test, and if he can *schnorr* dinner from Rabbi Remorse Red Herring, hitherto the most formidable and impregnable antagonist of the destitute, then he will be judged worthy to be Manasseh's son-in-law. The maiden's dowry would be "unique," as indeed it would, but not as Yankelé in his eagerness imagines. There would be all the money she gets from the synagogue which has money set aside for the dowries of portionless girls. There would be all of Manasseh's Jerusalem land, plus "some province or other in this country." When Yankelé gasps in happy anticipation, Manasseh loftily says, "Could I do less. . . . My own flesh and blood, remember!"

When Yankelé has withstood the ultimate challenge and has dined at the table of Rabbi Remorse, he naturally inquires after the promised dowry. It consists of non-existent assets. Money from the synagogue is awarded by lot and Deborah has nothing more than the same chance to get it as any other eligible girl. The Jerusalem property is a casket of Jerusalem earth, which Manasseh has preserved in his safe alongside his last will and testament.

Desperately Yankelé hopes that the English province is more tangible, but this is merely an agreement by

Manasseh that he will not himself *schnorr* in a certain area. They are to get a map of London on which in red pencil will be marked the domain in which Manasseh *schnorrs*. Yankelé is to choose a district within this area to be marked off in blue pencil; Manasseh will agree not to *schnorr* there himself, "from your wedding-day onwards." Once again we get the incongruous language of business negotiation for beggary, for religious activity, and for personal romance, crowned by the lofty assumption that a brokerage fee is in order. For the truth is, such a province is very valuable, and "under careful administration" its revenue might even be doubled or trebled. "I do not think your tribute to me need be more than ten per cent."

So in spite of everything he can do, Yankelé gets only the king's daughter, and he is grateful that she is herself not an item in the dowry. He should indeed be satisfied with so limited a victory, as he can hardly be a match for so keen a dialectician, one so used to getting his way by the shifts and dodges of specious argument.

Yet under no circumstances will Manasseh tell what might be described as a lie, and he reprimands Yankelé after his victory over Rabbi Remorse on the ground that he has been reduced to lying in order to prevail. Manasseh must lay it down that "A first-class *Schnorrer* never lies." He can indulge in any amount or variety of ingenious half-truths, fallacious arguments, and distinctions, but he must never tell an outright lie.

Manasseh exasperates the Mahamad partly by some verbal quibbling over whether he has consented to his daughter's marriage already or whether he only "meditates" consenting! This is like his favorite devices of division and subdivision of labor and function, by the aid of which he can get more money out of Grobstock by multiplying the things he expects to be paid for. When the ridiculous dispute over who is to get the precious salmon, whether indeed Grobstock has not stolen the fish from Manasseh who has in fact bought it with money that he has already fleeced Grobstock of—when this has gone far enough, Grobstock offers to pay Manasseh as much as he would have paid Jonathan the fishmonger for it.

This invites a distinction between profit and compensation as Manasseh exercises to the full his dialectical adroitness. Spurning Grobstock's offer of three guineas for the fish, Manasseh asks, "What of my profit? . . . Since you have made me a middle-man, since you have forced me into the fish trade, I must have my profits like anybody else." When another crown is offered, Manasseh goes on to demand "compensation" for at least two things, and his "tone assumed the sing-song sacred to Talmudical dialectics." He wants to be compensated for "not eating the salmon myself," as Groucho Marx asks of the musician, "How much do you get for not playing?"

After all, the salmon was only entrusted to Grobstock, and is it not ordained in Exodus that when a man turns over anything to his neighbor to keep he shall receive double for any loss or trespass? The second claim is even more impressive, and brings us back to the second level of his demand upon charity, his scholarship. The claim is, "Compensation for being degraded to fishmongering. I am not of those who sell things in the streets. I am a son of the Law, a student of the *Talmud.*"

More effective still in Manasseh's impressive equipment are his devices of evading the question and, almost by professional requirement, begging the question.

By ignoring Grobstock's implied charge that a beggar has no right to purchase a luxury like salmon, Manasseh makes it seem as if the philanthropist has recommended a crime. "You—you—rogue! How dare you buy salmon!" The retort is instantaneous, "Rogue yourself. . . . Would you have me steal salmon?"

Again he ignores Grobstock's charge and turns it to his own justification when he hears that he is a pauper and a beggar who has no business spending two guineas, all he has in the world, on a mere luxury. The answer is, "If I do not buy salmon when I have two guineas. . . . when shall I buy salmon?" Manasseh agrees that it is a luxury, and it is only on such rare occasions as this that he has the money to buy it! Poor Grobstock feels that there must be some reply to make, but he of course cannot think what it is. His silence enables Manasseh to complete his victory; he demands an apology, "to clear my good name which you have bespattered in the presence of my very tradesmen." So once again the mere rich man is overwhelmed by combined aristocracy and intellect.

Yankelé is not so readily vanquished, and registers an ingenious pun when his own chicanery is exposed. Manasseh finally admits that if he were to give Yankelé his daughter "You would thereby have approved yourself a king of *Schnorrers,* of a rank suitable to my daughter's, but an analysis of your argument will show that you are begging the question." The answer is exactly right for a profession based on fallacious reasoning to begin with. Yankelé simply asks, "Vat more proof do you vant of my begging powers?" All *schnorring* begs the question by assuming as proved what indeed is a long way from being so—the *schnorrer's* right to charity and his worthiness to receive it in view of the means he takes to become an outlet for goodness in others.

Manasseh's whole life is then based on a mistake in logic of which he is either unaware or which he hopes by various devices to conceal from others. Again we see how, for all his practical sense, Manasseh loves victory at the intellectual level. This recalls the pathetic Tevyeh in Sholom Aleichem and how Jewish he was in being content to win out just in argument. He had great skill in arguing one way and acting in another; the more convincing his logic, the more probable it was that he would ignore it. He was satisfied with intellectual victory, since material success always seemed reserved for others anyway.

As Zangwill has implied further in Manasseh's case, his ingenuity has been developed by training in the *Talmud,* where close reasoning and sharpness of mind for clearing up vexed questions are called for. We are brought back to a special quality in Jewish humor which so often shows something intellectually quick, a triumph of acuteness of mind over the actual facts and grim situations of life. Things always seem to be bad, are indeed endurable only if words and the mind can be made to triumph over them, to minimize or to find in them a twist, an element of relief or humor which obscures the hopeless wretchedness of things as they are. So the Jews have been able better to accept life in the face of what it has done to them.

But Manasseh not only towers above others by force of mind but achieves an independent income as well. He is one Jew who will not be content with mere intellectual victory, and the final episode which earns him his royal title draws together and exercises all sides of his genius.

His conquest of the formidable Mahamad was impressive, since this high and mighty council gave its consent to mixed marriages between Sephardim and Ashkenazim only with the greatest reluctance. While it is true that the Mahamad had less control over the marriage of a Sephardi woman with a Tedesco, it was not until 1706 that such a marriage had taken place, and later in the 18th century every possible discouragement was offered to similar unions.

Actually, the Mahamad had not met following Manasseh's dramatic appearance; the president was still prostrate after his stroke, and consent to the marriage was obtained from other synagogue authorities. Deborah was to have a proper Sephardic marriage and Yankelé was to have all the honors of a bridegroom. Now, on the last Sabbath before the wedding, Yankelé was to be called to a Reading of the Law before the congregation, preceded by his prospective father-in-law who would then make a customary offering to the synagogue.

The minister intoned, "The good name, Manasseh, the son of Judah, the Priest, the man, shall arise, to read in the Law," and so the great aristocrat strode magnificently to the reading platform and performed with the majesty and assurance of one to the manner born. Then came the hushed moment when the master reader announced Manasseh's gifts. A natural human curiosity always obtained as to how much would be given, and it was assumed that a mere *schnorrer* would be content to offer a very small sum.

The whole scene of Manasseh's public contribution suggests the religio-human duality in Zangwill's book and in Jewish life generally. One's piety cannot escape public opinion, and generosity is subtly prodded by what others are going to think of one's social status and character.

At last the figure of Manasseh's first contribution for charity in honor of Yankelé is heard—it is the incredible figure of five pounds. "A thrill ran through the building. Men pricked up their ears, incredulous, whispering to one another." But this is the merest beginning; Manasseh reels off one five-pound gift after another, until the gaze of the entire congregation is upon him as he stands impassive, scattering largesse as befits a royal figure. "It was indeed a kingly munificence, a sovereign graciousness," generously expanded to include all officials and dignitaries of the synagogue, beginning with the president of the Mahamad himself now unhappily absent because of illness. The final total reaches the unprecedented and staggering sum of a hundred pounds.

Now of course Manasseh does not have a cent of the money he has just promised to give. The next day he goes forth to collect it, and naturally looks first for his ancient victim Grobstock. This vigilant philanthropist, however, from an upper window sees Manasseh coming and makes his escape by a back door. He is only temporarily safe, however, and will be run to earth in final surrender. Meanwhile Manasseh waits upon one great Sephardi after another, getting contributions by his usual methods and refined arguments, appeals to pride and honor, religion, ancient usage, and noblesse oblige. His attack on the president of the Mahamad himself is a triumphant summary of his character and method as he refuses to let his honor and principle be set aside.

On hearing that the hundred pounds of debt to the synagogue are only Manasseh's own pledges, the president relaxes and feels that no harm is done if money that no one expects to get anyway is not forthcoming.

But he is overwhelmed as Manasseh in bitter astonishment makes use of his standard series of questions to which there can be only discreditable answers.

"Do you hold words spoken solemnly in Synagogue of no account? Would you have me break my solemn vow? Do you wish to bring the Synagogue institutions into contempt?" And then an invitation to heaven itself to strike once more the faithless one. "Do you—a man already once stricken by Heaven—invite its chastisement again?" The inevitable quotation from Scripture follows the demand that the president implore the forgiveness of God and make good Manasseh's debt in token of his remorse, "as it is written, 'And repentance, and prayer, and charity avert the evil decree.' "

When the money is still refused, Manasseh recalls that the synagogue will be profaned and "Even the Benediction which I in all loyalty and forgiveness caused to be said for the recovery of the President of the Mahamad is to be null, a mockery in the sight of the Holy One, blessed be He!" This familiar combination of the personal and religious puts the president so far in the wrong that in the end he gives Manasseh the five pounds which had been pledged for his recovery.

In like manner Manasseh wheedles and extorts money from a series of victims including his cousin Barzillai who is completely obfuscated by the refinements of logic, distinction of terms, and functions of which Manasseh is so great a master. A particularly absurd passage describes Manasseh's descent on the extravagant fop, Beau Belasco, who cannot afford charity because his way of life is so extravagant. By loftily pretending to find that the Beau's clothing is out of fashion, Manasseh gets him to discard a magnificent wardrobe which he then sells for the benefit of the synagogue.

But it is the defaulting Grobstock who must be cornered in the end, and so the episodic tale resumes its first encounter. Manasseh discovers his quarry in Sampson's Coffee House, hiding behind a broad sheet. Desperately Grobstock wants to know why he should be the victim, why other men equally rich should not be approached. The answer is that Manasseh would not think of advising Grobstock as to the proper method of investing money; he prefers to mind his own business which is *schnorring* and he knows best from whom he should try to get money.

"Trust me, I know best whom to come to. You stick to stocks and leave *Schnorring* alone." Grobstock is now faced with a barrage of Manasseh's usual arguments, specious distinctions, and appeals. It is in vain; Grobstock refuses even to give the five pounds vowed on behalf of Yankelé, "one of your own people." The magnate disdains to pay in honor of a "dirty *Schnorrer*" like Yankelé, and so offends Manasseh grievously. This is surely no way to speak of one who has been a guest in your house.

"Do you forget that Yankelé has broken bread at your table?" Still Grobstock is adamant, but finally wavers when the supreme humiliation faces him of having Manasseh arise and try to pay for his own coffee. The majestic figure now threatens to abandon his benefactor, but even here a distinction must be made. "I am done with you," said Manasseh. "I am done with you as a philanthropist. For the future you may besnuff and bespatter your coat as much as you please, for all the trouble I shall ever take. As a financier, I still respect you, and may yet come to you, but as a philanthropist, never."

There must have been an answer to this, but again

poor Grobstock cannot think what it is. "Anything I can do . . ." he begins to mutter vaguely, and he is lost. Manasseh persuades him to run the sixty pounds he has collected into six hundred, and so realizes enough to pay back the original debt, and to establish a fund for a suitable member of the congregation. It all turns out to be sanctioned by the highest authority. The original Ascamot of 1663 provides that voluntary offerings may be disposed of according to the donor's wishes; he may name the actual recipient of the charity, if he has himself given once before to the congregation's general funds. So Manasseh, as befits a learned aristocrat devoted to the strict practice of the Jewish religion, is in keeping with the most ancient law of his own synagogue in stipulating that the beneficiary of "the da Costa Fund" should be none other than himself.

Manasseh's last victory which placed him beyond the need of further beggary reminds us again of how purely Jewish he was. He clung fiercely to what had come down from the past, and showed no sympathy with new progressive trends in the Sephardic community. The old days when religion had to be cherished in secret or practiced at the risk of torture and death had inspired a devotion to its absolute letter, a practice of its rules with austere rigidity. A newer generation being freer and less afflicted were less inclined to follow a way of life which had once seemed beyond question. The outside world intruded more and more, the Sephardim blended in with native English practice, and the precious old inheritance was cherished by the few who were steeped in tradition or who came to it fresh from worse conditions elsewhere.

In time new generations came on who were not foreigners in England as the original community was; these were native Englishmen like any others and could hardly be expected to resist the inevitable. There was bound to be a decline in the old Sephardic scholarship and the uncompromising spiritual devotion to inherited law and practice. These pure ancient standards lose ground among Jews who necessarily go out into the rest of the world.

So it is left to an aristocratic beggar to uphold what others are becoming too weak, too worldly, too unJewish to sustain. Manasseh, the real aristocrat deeply rooted by blood, learning, and religion in the past, would not think of following the likes of Grobstock and besmirching himself in the concerns of the outside world. He never forgets that he is Jewish nor ever shows a sign that it even occurs to him to be otherwise. Here his devotion becomes practical once more, because in any other context he would have to give up being a *schnorrer*. His whole life, character, and mode of living depend on his remaining in the Jewish scheme of things, where alone the assumptions he makes are conceivable. In some ways he seems urbane and cosmopolitan, superior to any label or classification, but only by clinging to his especially intensified Jewishness can he go on combining his fabulous talents with profitable beggary.

And his ingenious defense of professional *schnorrerism,* which makes Grobstock feel uncertain and inferior, at times is so persuasive that we have to wonder whether it might not contain some truth after all. Manasseh shows that their positions, that the one has money and the other begs, are only passing material accidents, and if society refuses to assign value to the beggar's role he will have to assert some value for it. It is of course incongruous that one in so low a social state should adopt a superior attitude, and this becomes very funny.

But there is nothing laughable in the long history of poverty, injustice, and degradation that beggary implies; yet the beggar too is a man and must have his dignity, which ought to be higher and clearer than it is among other men.

To make it better, the *schnorrer* exaggerates and turns it completely around to make his human point. He builds up his position to equalize it with another's which is for the moment vastly superior. Some way has to be found to put Grobstock in the wrong and Manasseh in the right on human grounds, when clearly society and life in the world have greatly elevated one and depressed the other. The world's assumptions have to be upset to put down a rich and successful man below a wretched tramp. This is done by making the beggar enormously superior in all the ways that are supposed to suggest that one man is actually better than another, while at the same time showing that such superiority has nothing to do with worldly success, that in fact such success may well be achieved by men who have not a fraction of Manasseh's genius.

The whole becomes an ironic commentary on the absurdity of all human arrangements; one becomes almost persuaded that Manasseh is right, that his parasitical impudence and refusal to work for what he extorts from the sober, reasonable, and industrious pedestrians who have money and run the world—that this is in fact justified and is no more absurd than the actual nature of things.

"Tränen-Trieschke . . . Grünlich . . . Permaneder"

Manasseh is a brilliantly resolved paradox, and the reader is led, not to a willing suspension of disbelief in a seemingly pretentious swindler, but to the reluctant persuasion that Manasseh has a right to demand his livelihood at the expense of an inferior world. As Micawber was comic in failure, Manasseh is a laughable success.

Now the prosperous world of Thomas Mann's *Buddenbrooks* will begin amid the ease and gayety of success. With comic exuberance, playfulness, and delicate mockery of a number of human weaknesses Mann leads us gradually toward failure and decline, the defeat of all attempts at improvement, while our responses change with the fate of those commanding our sympathy. The comic elements cease to amuse us when they begin to undermine individual happiness as with the gloomy preachers and Tony's dreadful husbands, or to lead us into the family's decline as with Grünlich at first, and finally into the sad ineptitude of little Hanno.

Once, in answer to a question, Thomas Mann made the conventional distinction between humor and irony: humor shows a less intellectual and objective laughter than irony, "*das herzaufquellende Lachen*" is warmer and more humane. Mann is happy when readers find him more of a humorist than an ironist; indeed he is growing bored by constant reference to the irony that dominates his work.

By now his vast achievement has been studied and interpreted in thousands of books and articles, and recently the undiminished power of his later career has offered problems of great complexity to criticism. While *Buddenbrooks, "ein Buch pessimistischen Humors"* in Mann's own phrase, remains the most popular and accessible of the great novels, it has seemed to demand less recent attention than the output of fifty years later.

To be followed by *Der Zauberberg,* the Joseph tetralogy, and the all-but-incredible *Dr. Faustus,* to mention only the summits, would make any novel seem a minor work, and its comic aspect, however delightful at times, must seem lost amid the sombre tones not only of Mann's highest achievements in the later works, but in the tragic decline of the Buddenbrook family itself. Mann is praised for being the poet of death, of our common sorrow, of loss and bereavement; the reader of those unforgettable pages that tell of the death of Joachim Ziemessen, or the sacrifice of Rachel in giving life to Benjamin, will acquiesce. In *Buddenbrooks* itself the death of Tom displays a fearful power from which there can be no recovery.

But death is not the only mark of decline and fall in this masterpiece of a youthful writer, barely twenty-five. If we recall the dreadful tension as Tony's father examines the financial records of the bankrupt Grünlich; the well-nigh unbearable quarrel scene between Tom and Christian after their mother's death, while Tony in agonies of grief and shame constantly reminds them of the dead body in the very next room; the final tableau with its Euripidean lamentation of the eight women clothed all in black—recalling these and other moments of comparable grandeur, we might well pass over the comic element, content with our riches.

And yet as one begins the account of little Tony's lesson in catechism and moves into the family life, a certain tone as of amused detachment, a way of looking at things and people and presenting their lives, seems to emerge with a subtly comic effect. In a kind of Dickensian exuberance or excess, a love of seemingly irrelevant but vivid detail, an eye for the various forms of affectation or pretense, of hypocrisy, of ignorance, professional pomp and vanity, of the clash between what is professed and what is done, between the pretended and the real—in all these classical forms wherein comic discernment has declared itself, we find *Buddenbrooks* rich and full to our delighted astonishment.

But the exact nature of Mann's humorous posture undergoes so many and complex changes, and moves with such subtlety back into the sombre outlines of the work as a whole, that we shall find him elusive, as he wishes. We shall meet a blending of several attitudes as the forms of our common human weakness pass before his eye: affectionate sympathy, scornful antagonism, or more likely tender pity—all somehow related to amused indifference, as of one keeping himself at a distance from the object, ever above his creation so as to see it as it really is and only rarely becoming one with it when the movement toward decline and fall must have its way.

The book opens with genial gayety and the harmlessly mocking laughter of a sweet old man, Johann Buddenbrook, who is amused by the catechism lesson of his grandchild, Tony. A playful amusement is joined by his wife and daughter-in-law, as we find ourselves drawn into the life of the family, with its assured prosperity and serenity in the year 1835. Dealing as it does in people and their daily relationships, the novel is bound to contain studies of character and behavior in typical human situations wherein so much of the comic shows itself—those clashes and incongruities that make up the endless variations of human absurdity.

And like all novels of family life, *Buddenbrooks* contains a great many meals; the family table with its activity becomes a principal means of portraying character, the family atmosphere and its habits, the tone of succeeding generations. Like Dickens, Mann invests these occasions with a kind of excitement and fascination until we read with avidity every detail of what was consumed and the manner of serving it. In fact, the richness of what Orwell sees as irrelevant but interesting detail in Dickens is soon obvious as we become involved in Mann's similarly inexhaustible creative invention—an energy of imagination that continues throughout his career and is marked in *Dr. Faustus* as well.

Here in *Buddenbrooks* it delights us constantly from Herr Stuht, the tailor, whose belly was clothed in a wool shirt and fell with astonishing roundness over his breeches, to the speck of powder to be seen on the wart on the left nostril of the bridegroom, Bendix Grünlich; and the thin nose of the old retainer Grobleben, from which at all seasons there hung a long drop of something that never actually fell off.

At the great dinner in celebration of a magnificent new family mansion, we read with mounting excitement of the colossal, brickred ham, the shallot gravy, the masses of vegetables on such a scale that one might have satisfied his appetite from a single dish. The solemn function of carving, *das Tranchieren* is taken over by Lebrecht Kröger with uplifted elbows and index fingers stretched out precisely on the back of knife and fork, he cuts with deliberation the juicy slices one by one. The masterpiece of Konsulin Buddenbrook, *der Russische Topf,* is then passed and we savor a rich and pungent mixture of fruit conserves, meanwhile seated on heavy chairs, using heavy silverware, and drinking heavy wine. We share the obvious satisfaction of Herr Hoffstede, as he shoves into his mouth, his brows elevated, a single fork on which are accumulated ham, brussels sprouts, and potato. We see the general astonishment at the capacity of Klothilde, a poor relation and the butt of family jokes throughout. She is emaciated, tough, patient, and hungry, consuming two enormous helpings of every course, with heaps of supplementary ingredients.

All is in vain, for Klothilde is destined to grow ever more gaunt and attenuated, unlike Herr Köppen who, after the vast *Plettenpudding* is served—a mixture of layers of macaroons, raspberries, biscuits, and custard—is obliged to resist the strong need to loosen some buttons of his vest. The gayety is finally suspended by nothing more solemn than the stomach ache of a small boy, Christian, who lies groaning in agony from an excess of flaming plum pudding especially prepared for the children, while the adults are heavily faced by the last course of butter, cheese, and fruit, to be followed still by coffee, cigars, and liqueur. Christian's affliction is diagnosed as a slight indigestion, and the family physician, Dr. Grabow, prescribes some children's powder, camomile tea, and a strong diet of pigeon and French roll—the same and only remedy, alas, that the old man suggests for all afflictions throughout, trivial or mortal.

At the regular Christmas dinner nearly forty years later, we observe the same vast amounts of food and drink narrated in occasional repetitions of the same language used at the outset; but the tone of exuberant comic excess no longer moves us to burst out laughing as when being tickled, for the sombre movement of the family's life must have its way.

Christian's stomach ache has given cause for both amusement and alarm, with the development of his character showing him as much the object as the source of ridicule. He is early distinguished from the more solid and promising Tom, destined to become *Konsul* and head of the family grain business. Christian is a gifted mimic, but moody and capricious, given to a variety of silly jokes, at times delighting and dismaying the family by his escapades. Once he terrifies the company at table by seeming to strangle on a peach stone; they are relieved when Christian recovers quickly, saying that he was only supposing what would happen if he swallowed the stone.

His performance in school is generally deplorable, and he early reveals his strong bent toward the theatre when he is smitten with love for a young actress and spends money on a bouquet of flowers for her. His imitations are full of *unwiderstehlicher Komik,* irresistible to the family as when he imitates the extravagant movement and gestures of an impassioned piano virtuoso; his long anecdotes and stories are wildly entertaining, and at his club he soon becomes a great favorite with his imitations and pointless tales. Yet it is not long before the prevailing laughter seems in danger of being at, rather than with Christian and, where the family is concerned, his lazy indifference to business threatens a hard-won stability and unity. His account of a typical day in his life as a businessman is a burlesque of his brother's serious dedication, and Christian seems never to lose a chance to make fun of business, or indeed work of any kind.

This gradually alienates his brother until what began as a form of harmless and exuberant horseplay becomes a source of estrangement between the brothers, a cause of decline and fall. Thus Christian jokes his life away, and the business is well rid of him when he departs for Hamburg in May 1857. His good-for-nothing cronies come to the station to see him off, amid much reminiscent laughter, presents of flowers and cigars, and a final joke at Christian's own expense. This was the gift of an emblem to decorate his coat lapel, celebrating his exploits in a local brothel. In later years, Christian is still able to entertain the family with wildly extravagant performances, by imitations in numerous languages and dialects, but suddenly breaking off and lapsing into gloomy silence, as if knowing deep within that his play has played out.

The movement of Tony's life from a normally mischievous childhood to a maturity marred by sorrow begins with delightful sympathy and tenderness. Mann's understanding of the children's world, and the aloofness, the detachment of his role as their creator, are joined to form an amusing incongruity between the insignificant smallness of their actions and the children's own belief in their importance. As a little girl Tony becomes the friend and rival of Julchen Hagenström with whom she engages in splendid contests of boasting on the way to school. Julchen's brother Hermann is occasionally pleased to join them, and Tony is soon fascinated by the possible taste of a special kind of roll which Hermann carries in his lunch box. This creation is soft and oval in shape, citrus flavored, and containing currants as well, over which Hermann is pleased to lay slices of tongue or goose-breast.

When Tony longed to have a taste of this exotic combination Hermann of course demanded a price, a kiss in fact, which he then impetuously dared to collect. The ensuing struggle was interrupted by Julchen, who burst forth from behind a tree, tore off Tony's hat, and scratched her cheeks most lamentably. We are told simply that after this event, there was virtually an end to the *Kameradschaft*.

Tony's further behavior leaves much to be desired, given her bold and inquisitive nature, a certain proud and impudent assurance that involves her in various escapades. She goes about the town like a little queen, friendly or cruel, according to her taste or mood. On returning from a sojourn with her mother's family, the Krögers, Tony seems ever more unruly and vain. She is caught reading *Mimili,* a questionable book, and she has been seen out walking alone with a school friend of her brothers'. When this is forbidden, she carries on a secret correspondence in a hollow tree, so that finally at the age of fifteen Tony is placed under close supervision in the boarding school of Fräulein Sesemi Weichbrodt.

So far we are touched and amused as Tony's mischievous young life unfolds, the narration offered in a tone the most delicately comic, as we join in the kindly smile of Tony's creator.

The years wander past, and Tony's generally happy youth remains untroubled, until one lovely afternoon in early summer. As the family sit reading and talking in the garden after their coffee, the servant Anton appears with a calling card on the tea tray, announcing the arrival of one Grünlich, agent. There now appears the first in the series of men in Tony's life who seem at first glance preposterous in manner or behavior yet who in the end make of her life a scene of unhappy waste and loss. Grünlich is a man of medium height in his early thirties with thin, light blond hair and a rosy, smiling face somewhat disfigured by a striking wart on one side of his nose. Although his chin and upperlip are shaven, he wears a set of mutton-chop whiskers or *Favoris,* yellow gold in color.

We should think here of Lucian's suspicion of all conspicuous gravity, especially if it wears a beard; but now we are interested in making Grünlich's acquaintance as he comes forward with an air of submissive amiability. As his character develops we get a sense of one presenting a carefully planned façade, of one serious in business, constantly engaged in energetic activity, the *rastlose Tätigkeit* which he never ceases to emphasize. After professing his industrious zeal in a flourishing business, he expresses admiration for the conspicuous virtues of the Buddenbrook family, for the goodness, Christian virtue, and spirit that constitute his own ideal.

A note of pious intimacy with divine providence now creeps into Grünlich's discourse, and we long to cry out to Tony's unsuspecting parents to beware: to the eye of comic discernment, an explicit religious profession on the surface of any character must imply the opposite deep within. To his piety Grünlich adds the love of flowers, admiration for the beauties of nature, and constant praise of everyone and everything. He makes ingratiating inquiry after each one present and praises Christian's name so as to mention the implied holiness of his own—for Bendix is of course derived from Benedict, a name charged with blessedness and monastic austerity, a name borne by his ancestors of the pastoral calling.

He now inquires after Christian's studies, is delighted to hear that he is reading Cicero, praises the Latin classics and adds a bit of quotation to show his learning —this with a slight cough or clearing of the throat which gives a further impression of carefully rehearsed performance. He finds himself in complete agreement with everything said by Tony's parents, and then in a convenient lull he turns to her as next in line for praise and declares himself carried away by the beauty of her hair in the afternoon sunlight. With elaborate politeness and considerate apprehension lest he be intruding, Grünlich is called again by his *Tätigkeit* to take his departure, but is struck dumb with gratitude on receiving an invitation to take pot-luck with the Buddenbrooks during his stay in the city. The final note of one studying to give a certain impression of himself and his status is carried by a casual reference to the *paar Zimmer* he occupies at his hotel—not just one room but a suite of two as befits his place in the world.

After the stiff formality of his departure, Tony shows her direct insight into Grünlich's mixture of absurdity and selfish calculation. Christian imitates him with devastating effect, since Grünlich is so plainly an abstracted play-actor. But the *Konsul* dismisses their young realism, and draws together the impression that Grünlich had striven so hard to achieve, into a series of four adjectives: Grünlich is a Christian, able, industrious, and cultivated young man, the order and pomp of the German epithets having just the right air of pretentious formality to suit Grünlich's determined hypocrisy.

Despite the studied insult of Tony's reply to him on

a chance meeting in the street, he appears for Sunday dinner, rosy and smiling with carefully groomed *Favoris.* He falls upon a magnificently ample six course dinner with enthusiastic praise for every item, being unable in the end to resist asking for a second helping of the pudding. His conversation maintains the ingratiating deference to all and sundry of his first appearance, and he seems undismayed by Tony's studied indifference, her sarcastic response to his advances. He works steadily away at the portrait of himself as an ideal union of Christian goodness, business success, and worldly cultivation. When Tony hears from her father eight days later that Grünlich has asked for her hand in marriage, his image rises before her still in all of its pretentious absurdity, and she declares a scornful refusal.

Grünlich's behavior is studied, careful, calculated; if one is looking for them, the stigmata of Fielding's theory of hypocritical affectation soon emerge. But Grünlich quickly passes beyond any comic tolerance despite the ludicrous effect of his appearance. Still in the impassioned discourse which he delivers to Tony when they are alone, amid its fearful implications for her there intrudes an incongruous note. Her name, he cries, with indelible letters is written on his heart, "*geschrieben.*" No, he suddenly corrects himself and says rather "*gegraben,*" that is dug or engraved forgetting that, while this has a more serious meaning on the surface, it suggests burial as well. So the insincerity of a speech which has been clearly memorized and rehearsed for the occasion is exposed.

Tony now finds herself looking closely at his features, as he takes her hands and stares into her eyes: the red face, the wart on his nose, the blue eyes—blue as those of a goose. The very features that on first sight were laughable take on a sinister aspect before Tony's painful aversion. She is left in tearful exhaustion, but Grünlich is not to be denied. When he chooses to interpret Tony's response as a form of encouragement he sends her a ring, with a letter referring to himself in the third person as *"Endesunterfertigter,"* a kind of Micawberesque use of the undersigned in a tone of legal detachment. But when he learns of Tony's affair with young Morten Schwarzkopf, Grünlich hastens to the scene to declare his rights. On first seeing him Morten, like almost everyone else, can barely keep a straight face before the red, gold-yellow, and blue now so familiar to us.

But there is nothing laughable about the product of Grünlich's appearance, unless it is the autocratic finality of Morten's father, the sudden, pompous, and humorless word with which he puts a lifelong end to Tony's only chance for happiness: it is all a futile childsplay, *"und damit Punktum!"* Later on we cannot help a rueful smile at the engagement itself which lacks the fire and intensity of the proposal; Grünlich is content to seal the engagement with a discreet kiss upon Tony's brow in the company of her parents. A few reserved advances in private complete the courtship, and on his wedding day Grünlich appears with an air of calm possession—his face red, the whiskers groomed, and that little excess of powder visible on the wart of his left nostril. The ceremony proceeds by order and usage, but Grünlich has to clear his throat before saying *ja* to the final question; after this there is a massive consumption of good food, and Tony is doomed.

Her life is unrelieved until the unspeakable villainy of her husband comes to light, and she returns home once more. When their only child is born, a slight dispute as to her name is settled in favor of Grünlich's choice, Erika—a half-comic revelation of the man's pompous autocracy, as if there were any chance of an opinion other than his own prevailing.

Tony's first marriage ends in failure, she returns home with Erika, and assumes her place in the family circle once more. After the death of Uncle Gotthold we read of a family gathering on the traditional Thursday, and of the presence of the three unmarried daughters of Gotthold who are not slow to remark with accustomed sharpness upon any sign of weakness or failure in other members of the family. We become aware of the great distance between harmless comic enjoyment and the cruel mockery of deliberate malice in these bitter creatures who see matter to condemn in everyone down to the innocent little Erika whose growth is held to be retarded and who displays an alarming resemblance to her father, the perfidious Grünlich.

But as the years go on Tony finds life at home monotonous, particularly as the religious obsession of her mother intensifies with age and the daily devotions at home grow ever more fierce and prolonged. Tony endures the exercises as best she can, but one morning a particularly odious hymn, sung with words of embarrassing crudity and unconscious metaphorical absurdity, is too much for her, and she throws the hymn book away out of inner contrition—"*Zerknirschung,*" a delightfully ambiguous word.

Still Tony was compelled to attend the *Jerusalemabend,* a pious exercise established by her mother for the benefit of missionary work abroad. Some twenty ladies, of an age when one is inclined to look about for a secure place in heaven, would gather once a week for the reading of holy hymns and treatises, during which useful handwork would be done, the whole accompanied by delicious helpings of food and drink. The concern for heaven seems to have deepened as the ladies neared the time of entering it, but the enjoyment of good things here and now was not forgotten in the zealous pursuit of salvation and the doing of good works. Mann's ridicule of the entire superstition is here, as if anything could be more absurd than to suppose that heaven was a local habitation containing specific places, like reserved seats in a railroad compartment, the whole indicating the intellectual level of the ladies who were capable of believing it.

This concern for heaven is the more ludicrous in being fairly recent, something not pressing while the ladies were young or unlikely to die, but coming on only now that old age is near, an inconsistency that they were too stupid to see or were afraid to admit.

The commentary on these Jerusalem evenings keeps a tone of amused detachment and delicate mockery, as Mann stays far above his subject and so affords a tolerant smile.

He describes the membership with relish, including a wrinkled little creature named Himmelsbürger, rich in the favor of God and crochet patterns who, being the last of her family, described herself as indeed the last citizen of heaven. We meet as well the two eccentric old maids, the Gerhardt twins with their remarkable union of spiritual knowledge and insight, pious quotations, predictions, and good works. Of these the deaf one, Lea Gerhardt, is official reader to the circle, but to hear herself she must read in a fearful voice, sounding like the wind in a stovepipe to long-suffering ears. Tony's response to Lea's fear lest Satan should devour her is a most earthly question: will she ever become as ugly as these scarecrows?

In time this heavily laden piety is burdensome to the house and family, especially when a great series of pastors and missionaries, in long hair and black clothes, pass through for the collection of money and the consumption of vast quantities of expensive food.

On one occasion Tony could not help playing a joke on one conspicuous consumer to whom she served an uneatable stew. She grumbled audibly at people who eat widows out of house and home, and began to hate these black-clothed gentlemen bitterly. As comic types, these are among the hills of flesh with the massive, tubercular appetites of the pious, recalling Mr. Stiggins of Pickwickian fame and the holy ones of *Bleak House*. As in Tony's first suspicions of Grünlich, the sight of long black garments, solemn faces, and uplifted eyes made her question the virtue within, and inspired the malice of her sarcastic reply to the missionary Jonathan —a man with large, reproachful eyes and sad, low-hanging jowls—who desired to know whether the careful grooming of her forelocks might be consistent with true Christian modesty. Jonathan forgot that in his own Micawberesque baldness he was vulnerable to Tony's rapier question, whether she might beg the pastor to concern himself with his own ringlets?

Her sufferings among the holy guests of her mother allow Mann to display his masterly economy, an infallible deftness of stroke, letting the portrait of a single human being emerge in a few lines, as in Dickens. The triumph of this compression is Pastor Tränen-Trieschke from Berlin, a creation worthy of Boccaccio, Fielding, or Dickens, who appears to us in one supremely vivid paragraph. His nickname comes of a fervent religious emotion causing him to burst into tears in the midst of his sermon every Sunday.

Now he stays with the Buddenbrooks eight or ten days, vies with Klothilde in absorbing enormous meals, conducts pious devotions for the family and, despite the existence of a wife and many children in Berlin, falls in love with the countenance and still blooming figure of Tony. Again, carried away by emotion, the pastor does not weep, but writes a letter that mingles Biblical quotation and remarkably ingratiating tenderness, causing the same to be delivered by Anton to Tony's bedroom.

Rarely must we regret that something is missing from the text in a work by Thomas Mann, the most thorough of writers, concerned to exhaust the whole of every experience before he has done with it. But we now long for a copy of this letter in full, shown quickly to her mother by the indignant Tony. Disillusioned again before the realities of masculine hypocrisy, Tony utters the first of a series of half-comic outcries in which, with the force of a trumpet blast, her bitterness is summarized in the names of the men, mostly swindlers, who have betrayed her. Thus far, only one name compels remembrance, declaring all that she has learned of perfidy and pious hypocrisy is in "Grünlich."

Tony's vigilance against an erring clergy at times leaves us uncertain of her own provocation, as when in her letter from Munich she reports that a high episcopal figure driving by in a coach made eyes at her with the boldness of a young lieutenant. But Tony is not alone in remarking the comic aspect of a minister whose outer performance cannot conceal a falsity within. The one who presides over the christening of little Hanno Buddenbrook is seen through the veiled mockery of Gerda's mysterious eyes, the child's mother. He belongs with the ministerial portraits, among the *schwarze Herrn* of

Tony's exposure, presenting one more clash between his ideal and the mechanical manner of his performance.

Mann's touch is infallible when describing a given company assembled for an occasion like the christening of Hanno. With his expert, sure strokes he portrays them as a whole and as individuals, each one singled out from the rest, his character and appearance isolated, the author at once creating and observing in a masterly command of imaginative resources. The concealment of weakness or some unlovely inner reality is impossible before an eye so penetrating and relentless, an intelligence so cool and aloof, a reading of human nature so charged with confident mockery. Now we meet and quickly see to the core, the man Andreas Pringsheim, *pastor marianus*. Although he bears the family name of the author's wife, the name as it comes forth in this company grows ever more telling as Pringsheim's own nature is deftly exposed: it comes to suggest his worldly, unctuous character, that is all things to all men, his ingratiating yet solemnly pious manner, all balance and calculation, the dexterous Capuchin perhaps of Gibbon's phrase.

Meanwhile, however, a new man has come into Tony's life in the person of one Alois Permaneder, at first sight the most Dickensian of the great portrayals in *Buddenbrooks,* an unconsciously headlong character bent only on being himself. Absurd in speech, figure, and action, he is never so wicked as Grünlich, but ends much as he begins—essentially formless, good-natured, and harmless, with a face somewhat like a sea-lion's.

On his first visit from Munich he introduces himself to Tony's mother after apologizing for having no personal card. His voice is loud, his accent crude, the dialect so thick as to be barely comprehensible. His gestures are uninhibited, as of one not used to the reserve and self-possession of formal society. Having a number of nervous tics, he rubs his knees, sighs loudly, and makes wide circular gestures in the air. He seems a kind of preposterous social mistake, something that has been attempted but abandoned before completion as not having quite succeeded. Thus his voice, speech, and behavior are exactly those suggested by his somewhat formless and undisciplined appearance. He is clearly a man who has become what he is absent-mindedly, without thinking about it—his face, figure, voice, and manner all the result of forgetfulness by one who never had realized that there was anything to think about in such matters, to be curbed or adjusted by an outside standard.

When Tony comes in, Permaneder seems unable to stop moving, in contrast to his later *unverdrossenen Seszhaftigkeit,* indefatigable capacity to sit. Now he becomes a violent windmill of motion, gesticulation, and excited comment. When he is invited to stay for refreshments he accepts almost before the invitation is complete, as if expecting it; he is so fat that he must sit some distance from the table, but he finds himself very comfortable and soon takes out a huge pipe of fearful steam power that rapidly fills the room with smoke. His manner, almost incomprehensible speech, a certain formlessness of behavior, and a depressing amiability continue to astonish.

At last, after three hours, he begins to take his departure. The measure of his vulgarity is seen again in the spontaneous acceptance of a polite invitation to stay with the family rather than at his modest hotel; he will have his baggage sent 'round directly and will himself return when his business is transacted. It is now clear that the house and family are to be spared nothing; shaking his head and muttering grotesquely phrased compliments to Tony, Permaneder finally takes his clumsy departure.

When he moves into the house the already conspicuous qualities of this loud, shapeless, and incomprehensible provincial become fixed and obvious in everyone's view. To his unwearied stationariness he adds a habit of seeming to groan, not out of dismay but from an intensely deepening comfort and sense of smug well-being. Like some of the ecclesiastical visitors, he stays on in the house long after his business seems to be completed. He is clearly alien to the world of this patrician merchant family, yet he seems harmless, with none of the hypocritical knavery of his predecessor in Tony's life.

Events take their course and, after her second marriage, Tony goes to live with Permaneder in Munich. He soon discloses a variety of personal weaknesses that are not unanticipated and though he is still no villainous Grünlich, he shows a tendency to grumble and, on the other side of his *Formlosigkeit* and undisciplined amiability, an obstinate wilfulness, becoming an irresponsible self-indulgence. His evenings pass in the *Hofbräuhaus* drinking and playing cards with his cronies. He abandons all pretense of regular employment, deciding to live on Tony's dowry and his own property. Permaneder thus makes an undignified surrender and loses all sense of obligation to Tony and her family.

She now faces a life of hopeless monotony, of a depressing emptiness and dullness as her husband goes his own way, leaving her as much a stranger in his world as he was in hers. The crude lack of style might have been endurable, if Tony's last hope had not died with the loss of her new child, a girl that barely survives her birth.

Not surprisingly, considering the generally good-natured, but dull-witted fatalism with which Permaneder accepts the loss of his child, he returns after two or three days to his established way of life and his regular three pints at the *Wirtshaus* of an evening, showing the amiable, but thin, unsubstantial quality of his nature. Beyond this, however, he is guilty of a degree of infidelity revealed late one night when Tony is awakened by some unmistakable sounds on the stairway near her bedroom. A certain rustling, creaking, hoarse giggling, and scuffling place the matter beyond doubt, and Tony suddenly bursts upon Herr Permaneder attempting to kiss and embrace Babette, the cook, she meanwhile resisting his advances with something less than entire success.

Despite the painful implications of the scene in Tony's life, her agonized account of it seems irresistibly comic. The pomp and abstractness of the language make the events related appear trivial. A highly formal mode of discourse recounts something of little consequence, establishing the incongruity on which so much of the comic experience depends. Permaneder's antics become absurd when told so pompously by the narrator and received so violently and tragically by Tony.

At the moment of discovery, Babette profanely brings forth something like "*Jessas, Maria und Joseph,*" while Permaneder can do nothing but repeat the same after her in his consternation, "*Jessas, Maria und Joseph,*" as she disappears. This cry for succor to the holy family is at once an exclamation of fear, surprise, and dismay together with an anguished appeal for help from heavenly powers, all earthly assistance being now clearly in vain, even if at hand.

We must, to be sure, sympathize with Tony's fearful anguish and the bitter end to her last hope for personal happiness, yet the sudden intrusion of "*Jessas, Maria und Joseph*" is absurdly comic. Permaneder's first speech to the family had contained this peculiar dialect spelling, *Jessas,* and as now employed the change from "Jesus" suggests either another person than the revered Jesus of Christian tradition, his family sanctified by goodness that would never stoop to such behavior as that now exposed—or it implies a different version of Jesus, a person with a name spelled a little differently, to identify one called on for aid by evil-doers in their moments of crisis or exposure. Reeking now of alcohol after a long celebration of a friend's name day, Permaneder offers lame excuses to Tony sobbing on her bed, his halting dialect even more than ever preposterous under these conditions as a form of speech to convey meaning.

Now Tony's whole revulsion of feeling against her husband gets the better of her; things are said on both sides from which there can be no retreat or recovery, which no apology or contrition can hope to absolve. In another of the long dialogs between Tony and her brother Tom which carry so much of importance in the work as a whole, he pleads with her to take a dispassionate view of the affair. Yet Grünlich marries Tony to pay his debts, Permaneder to avoid work: both marry for money and neither loves her. Everything about them seems at first ridiculous, but they end as serious elements in the decline of the family.

But Tom, while willing to concede the impropriety, summarizes the harmless nature of Permaneder's offense: an excusable or at least understandable weakness to be forgiven. Charging that Tony does not take the matter comically enough, he tries to restore Permaneder to the comic tone and condition once more, wherein as throughout these readings so far, his weaknesses are seen for what they are but are accepted with a silent, kindly smile. Thus if Tony will be rather amused than indignant, she may even draw closer to her husband after all. He has made himself ridiculous, but if Tony will see this with the eye of comic tolerance rather than retributive justice, she will find her position happier than ever.

But she is adamant, insisting on divorce, and so the failure of her comic sense, of growing to maturity as Tom sees it, insures the failure of her life. This is a bagatelle and she ought to be relieved that it is nothing worse, yet she responds with bitter tears instead of shouting in relieved laughter. Her final outburst of enraged sensibility is not to be answered; her feelings pour out in a torrent of language before which the forms of dispassionate reason, of detached irony, are helpless. This too must then run its course, and at almost the exact half point of the book Tom is left alone to sustain the family's honor.

Alas, poor Tony, the narrator cries, as her life like the great book that contains her moves from a beginning in happy laughter to a scene of tearful mourning. Yet she remains half comic in her incongruous ideas, as Erich Heller says, something of a child without the knowledge of life she constantly professes to have learned. Her refrain of sorrow over what life has done to her, and what this has taught her of the earnestness of existence, has an air of self-conscious pride and satisfaction. She is naively deceived as to her own nature and survives all that fate can do against her, being in fact a little too stupid to realize the meaning of it.

Does she really believe all her outcries, assertions of

betrayal and suffering? It seems not, and so despite bravery and pride, she remains, in A. F. B. Clark's view, a muddle-headed failure. She sees nothing laughable in her lists of the odious men who have offended her—lists that begin with Grünlich alone and steadily increase in length as the number of *Filous* grows. Like the blasts of a trumpet, the litany of ecclesiastical hypocrites and worldly knaves sounds forth, the identity of her two husbands given as before, during and after marriage simply in their last names: "*Tränen-Trieschke . . . Grünlich! Permaneder! Tiburtius! Weinschenk! Hagenströms! . . . Was für Filous, Thomas.*"

A parcel of rogues in varying degrees perhaps, yet all beginning laughably, they come each to play his role in the sombre movement of the story and become one with its sorrow. One after another the comic elements move toward the doom that closes in upon the novel from all sides—symbolized in the mysterious, blue-tinted shadows about the eyes of Gerda and her only son. As Grünlich and Permaneder are lost in the sad failure of Tony's life, so we shall find the absurd school-teachers, their efforts at formal education, and all that is done in the name of health and well-being, to lose itself, obscurely and uselessly in the pathetic end of Hanno Buddenbrook.

Hanno, Kai,
and the "Oil of Sorrow"

Like Swift's A Tale of a Tub, Buddenbrooks addresses itself to abuses in religion and learning—rather to the absurdities that lie within all efforts at improvement of the obstinate realities of human nature. From the outset in chapter 2, when Tom and Christian come home from school and Christian, aged only seven, makes irresistible fun of the teacher Marcellus Stengel, Mann's treatment of school and its teachers is largely comic. Indeed almost all of the teachers introduced throughout the novel are ridiculous in some way, beginning with Stengel and the row of half a dozen sharp pencils protruding from his vest pockets, Pastor Hirte and his fondness for the coincidence of his name that means shepherd with his title, and all the others who contend with the likes of Christian—harmless and good-natured fellows as they were.

But apart from these to begin with, the mere statement of the curriculum sounds absurd. The tone of the German in announcing the subjects of Stengel's instruction has an air of abstractness, of that amused detachment by which Mann suggests how far from what is demanded by these subjects the pupil's performance is sure to be. Writing, figuring, singing, drawing—merely to list the subjects suggests that the whole notion of these or any like requirements must be absurd in that anyone should pretend to command them, that such a fellow as Stengel should pretend to teach them, or that such a young clown as Christian should be trying to learn them.

Thus Mann seems to find something inherently comic in the whole educational scheme of things, showing how preposterous it is to think that average human nature will come near to what is required, will overcome so dramatic a clash between the ideal and the real, between what is professed and what is in fact done once more —between the Bible extracts of Tränen-Trieschke and his lewd advances to Tony.

The attempted education of Hanno Buddenbrook is doomed to defeat even more certainly than that of the young rogue, Christian, however, and here the absurdities that Mann sees in the whole educational process take on a poignant tenderness as they become one with the sufferings of Hanno, emphasizing as they do how sadly out of place he is in the world.

When the usual adult question is put to him, does he like going to school, Hanno can only reply with a wearily resigned shrug. But one must learn reading, writing, figuring, "and so forth" Hanno interrupts to say, as if to ask in turn, who cares what the subjects are? He will never know what he is supposed to know about them, he can only remain indifferent to or accept patiently this and all the other mistaken efforts to do him good. Because he cannot learn arithmetic readily, he needs special instruction, obtained in this case from a tutor, a man with a red beard and unclean fingernails who waits for him in a hot room that smells unpleasant.

The red beard, the dirty fingernails, the odious room are signs of a threatening ugliness moving in upon the boy at the outset of his life when he is least able to oppose it. They mean that the world as it is will flow over his soul and finally destroy it. As he fails amid the absurdities of school and its preceptors, so must he fail in his life as a whole whose cruelties and usages he cannot sustain. Longing to devote himself to music he must now endure the heavy days at school amid the teachers whose punishment he fears while secretly despising them for their social inferiority, spiritual pettiness, and physical coarseness.

Amid this dreary futility Hanno meets another outsider who becomes his devoted friend, the little aristocrat growing up like an animal on his father's estate amid chickens, dogs, and vegetables, a delightful mass of incongruities, Kai Mölln. Kai is the son of Eberhard Graf Mölln, a widowed recluse who early insures his privacy by erecting a sign to this effect: "Here lives Count Mölln all by himself; he needs nothing, buys nothing, and has nothing to give away," thus defeating all the likely reasons for intrusion.

Losing his mother at birth, Kai leads a wild, neglected existence, but his unkempt appearance as he enters Hanno's life belies a superior nature seen in his face, brow, and eyes. His hands are dirty and he wears a shabby suit of uncertain color, missing buttons, and obvious patches on the seat. Despite this surface of dirt and haste and neglect, Hanno is drawn to Kai whom he meets at school and Kai responds with all the violence and energy of his untamed but gifted nature. If their teachers are inadequate failures, the two little fellows are equally certain to defeat the ideal of learning, each for different reasons, being hopelessly out of sympathy with the standard disciplines and requirements; their friendship is developed with the greatest care and tenderness, the serious account of their little world showing an infinite pity and understanding. As Kai comes daily for a joint attack upon their lessons, we respond to a touching description of their distracted grapplings with the problems of arithmetic, grammar, and spelling.

If measures taken for the benefit of Hanno's mind are sure to fail, so in turn all attempts to improve the boy's uncertain health fall short of their aim. Hanno learns early in life that everything beneficial is an agony, especially when Herr Brecht, the dentist, enters his life. The sessions with Herr Brecht leave Hanno half dead with terror, pain, and exhaustion, somewhat relieved by the parrot Josephus, who slightly resembles Herr Brecht in appearance and who provides some comic diversion by his voluble discourse.

The consolations of Josephus, however, can go only so far and when, in order to make Hanno's wisdom teeth possible, Herr Brecht has to remove four others that have already come in, Hanno lies eight days in bed, out of simple exhaustion and lassitude. But the dental agonies only aggravate other weaknesses of body and spirit that lead to fearful nightmares, sudden outcries in sleep as of one threatened by unspeakable terrors. These experiences shade into the sadly comic treatment to which Hanno is subjected when it is discovered that his blood is lacking in red corpuscles.

We meet again the ludicrous disparity between what is aimed at and what is accomplished, between the good intended and the suffering caused. A kind of weary pathos underlies the offhand report on the medicine prescribed, how it was administered and by whom, its hopeless futility when vomited up, the cure sadly worse than the disease, and the ineffectual doctors with their long history in the literature of the comic. We see the clash between the ignorant limitations of the doctors, their sober sincerity and zeal, the affectionate concern of Ida Jungmann and the family on one hand, and the actual fact in Hanno himself, his agonized response to it all, the irrelevance of this immense effort to what really ailed the boy and would finally make life impossible for him. The medicine was cod liver oil, to be taken from a porcelain spoon twice a day as it punctually was done, and at first as punctually vomited forth again. We think of the mathematical wafer in *Gulliver's Travels* designed to make learning easy, the proposition written on it with a cephalic tincture and borne up to the brain in digestion but vomited up instead by the perverseness of lads. Thus all that the world designed for Hanno's benefit was in fact rejected with unconquerable loathing by the obstinate, perverse reality of his nature.

But when in the course of time Hanno had grown used to cod liver oil it was further decided to regulate his digestion by good, thick, shining-silver castor oil taken from a table spoon, a wholesome remedy that slid down one's throat like a slippery lizard and remained for three days in the nostrils and gullet. Once Hanno had been greatly soothed by a prescription of arsenic pills, but of course these could not be repeated, being so pleasant, whereas cod liver and castor oil were known to all the world as wholesome. The pitiful homeliness of the remedy is caught in these two sad terms, like the "oil of sorrow" that tormented the young Thomas Carlyle, assaulting in vain his cast-iron peasant's constitution.

For Hanno the inadequacy of these available remedies emphasizes again the reason for their failure—the boy himself, so much a boy from (the young) Dickens, with all the world against him. The world starts from itself and not from what the boy is; he must accommodate to its demands and it will leave him alone. But Hanno cannot manage it: he hates doctors and their sorrowful oils, dentists and their hideous ministrations, school teachers and their threatening lessons.

His failure to improve physically becomes the more dramatic when contrasted with the triumphant success of the brothers Hagenström. If wholesome oil at two levels fails to improve his body, it is decided that he should avail himself of the athletic exercises directed by the teacher of gymnastics, Herr Fritsche, which provides opportunity for the manly youth of the city to show and develop the virtues of "*Mut, Kraft, Gewandtheit, und Geistesgegenwart*"—the fearful terms that resemble the subjects of an academic curriculum in their abstract remoteness from what the boy desires or is capable of. Courage, strength, dexterity, presence of mind—fine aims indeed but each in turn adding to Hanno's sufferings, his own sense of failure, and the perplexity of the doctors and his father.

In humiliating contrast to the ineptitude at all levels of Hanno and Kai, there is the shining example of two sets of Hagenström brothers, cousins of each other, and destined for all forms of success admired by the world.

We respond once more to the lucky perfection of this name, the same infallible accent that Mann so often attains with his best names. Pronunciation is important here, as Mann's German assumes an onomatopoetic quality with strong vowels and sharp consonants calling up the desired effect by aptness of sound. Even before we know the character well, the name seems a perfect choice, so that we are sure of the need for the name to be just what it is, as so often with Dickens. After we grow familiar with the character his name seems to take on his special qualities, so that Bendix Grünlich, we are sure, has to mean just that complex of scheming calculation and villainous hypocrisy revealed by its bearer.

And now the Hagenström boys could not be called anything else. Two of them are ambitious, of beehive industry, and consumed with longing to achieve the position of head boys to be number one in their classes. The others are two *Prachtkerle* indeed, splendid fellows of great muscular vigor, the finest gymnasts and swimmers in school, full of mischief and exuberant energy. To such as these, we are sure, the Hagenströms of the world, must come all honor and success.

By contrast Hanno and Kai are neither athletes, burly, dexterous, and daring fellows, nor students, industrious and eager to learn so as to stand with honor at the head of their class. When time comes for the gymnastic drills, Kai decides that there is no fun in it; hating any form of orderly discipline, he repeats a disdainful phrase used by his unsocial father, "*Hol's der Geier,*" and loftily consigns the wholesome exercise to the vultures. As for Hanno, he sets an impossible condition for his own attendance: if Herr Fritsche might not reek of beer and sweat on just one day, the thing could be discussed! Nothing is more tenderly, delightfully comic than the dismissal of the athletic director and his works by these cool, detached little fellows. Herr Fritsche stinks of sweat and beer, so they will have nothing to do with his exercises designed to perfect their bodily courage, alertness, strength, and dexterity.

As with organized gymnastics, so with winter sports and summer bathing, more of the doctor's remedies; they succeed with the ebullient Hagenströms who have no need of them, and fail with those for whose benefit they are intended. In the water and out of it, the Hagenströms prevail. They swim like sea-lions, swoop down on Hanno standing helpless in the pool, seize him in their muscular arms and force him down under the dirty water, holding him there until he understands his place in the world, letting him up finally to gasp for breath. Just once, however, Kai manages to take a wild revenge, swims underwater and fastens with all his teeth upon the leg of Hanno's tormentor, sending him home with a noticeable limp. But in winter or summer the water as the field of athletic contest is not the true home of our little men.

Having decided against Herr Fritsche, Hanno reminds Kai of their favorite indulgence—the telling of long stories of excited adventure, invented with marvelous energy by Kai, at the climactic moments of which, on the narrator's signal, Hanno breaks in with musical accompaniment. Now the story of that ring, found by Kai in a swamp at the bottom of a fearful abyss, has still a long way to go. Herr Fritsche and the Hagenströms are forgotten as the two friends escape into a world where they can be supreme.

If Hanno's body cannot profit from the remedies offered for its benefit, so must his mind and spirit reject their chance for development by means of formal education. In one of the longest chapters anywhere in the work of Mann, he describes a single day in the life of this most reluctant schoolboy. Mann has himself warned against seeing this chapter as nothing more than a satire on the German school system of its day. On the contrary, school here stands in the place of life itself, before whose mocking cruelty and custom the tardy child must shudder. Athletics, castor oil, and school are the ever-threatening, sinister evils in Hanno's life. If only he could have done with these, his body would end as strong as its nature would permit, his mind and spirit would be at peace, free to go their own way in realms of their own choice, to fulfill their possibilities, such as they were.

But the hour of reckoning comes: it is Monday morning and Hanno has done nothing about his lessons all week-end, carried into the empyrean as he has been by a performance of *Lohengrin*. A terrible rendezvous with the world as it is now faces Hanno, with something intended to do him good once more, and so bound to increase his sufferings. He knows that he should get up and prepare for the day, but it is so cold and dark, and perhaps he won't be called on after all.

Latin, Ovid that is, and chemistry—we need only to list these to see that like all statements of the curriculum the subjects Hanno should have studied declare that they will never be mastered, that what ought to be done will never be achieved, out of failure in will or sad incompetence.

The coming school day is another doomed absurdity then, as Mann vividly recreates Hanno's evasion and consolatory self-deception: if the regular alphabetical order is not followed, his turn won't come; why not just go on sleeping? So time passes, the precious hour set aside for the final preparation of lessons long postponed is gone, and now he must rouse himself. Work is out of the question and he can only hope to reach school on time; yet still he does not move, and steals another defiant five minutes as the cruel, unfeeling hands of the clock move on.

When at last he is up in the cold he must hurry. When he assembles the books needed for the day's recitations, the abstractness of their names—religion, Latin, chemistry—gives a further sense of remoteness, of their intrusive irrelevance for the chief bent of Hanno's life. In his desperation he now rushes through breakfast and, half-sick with anxiety, he runs off, in ironic haste to make certain of meeting his own failure. Far from having time to prepare lessons, he ends without time even to reach the school's opening exercise.

After an agonized effort, sweating and trembling, his heart beating irregularly, Hanno barely slips through the gate before it is closed. He misses the chapel exercise but plans to take his place in the classroom, acting as if nothing were amiss. He falls exhausted into his seat, resting his head on his outstretched arms. Hating the room, he is depressed by the coming dangers that it must contain; yet for the moment he is alone and at peace.

Suddenly he is aware of sounds of rustling at the rear of the room; turning quickly, he beholds the figure of Kai, Count Mölln, extricating itself from behind the last benches, dusting itself off, and coming forward with beaming countenance, greeting Hanno with relief in a cracking voice that clearly is in the process of changing. As in the comic relief at a mystery thriller, we are most grateful to Kai for thus breaking into the mood of tense anxiety and exhaustion—unchanged as he is in appearance with a kind of absent-minded improvisation—earthy, genuine, comic. He is happy to see Hanno in place of the "*Stück Lehrkörper*" or example of teacher in the flesh whom he has feared.

Having sneaked away from the morning service himself, Kai is greatly cheered and encouraged to find that Hanno knows as little as he does of what is required for the day. His explanation of why he has done nothing over the weekend is drily, ruefully amusing and may serve as the universal excuse for the Monday morning delinquent to the end of time: he did not work on Saturday because the next day was Sunday, and on Sunday he did not work on grounds of piety. Now there is little for the sluggards but to wait and accept what the day will bring, and all too soon they hear their comrades returning from the brief religious exercise that on Monday invokes the mercy of heaven upon the days to come.

The room fills quickly, the boys take their places led by the great Adolph Todtenhaupt, the head boy who has yet to miss a single question in his career as a student. Again we incline to burst out laughing at the astonishing energy and good luck of the boy's name, seeming to remove him further still from anything that Hanno or Kai could hope to be. Adolph is indeed all that our young friends are not and never can be: assured, diligent, thorough, coolly certain that all problems and demands are within his range—never threatened or fearful of the future, of what the world may ask of him.

Sitting near to Hanno, Adolph offers a greeting with a soft, malicious smile as he turns away for his final preparation, a smile that contains the entire mockery of the world as it is against Hanno's hopeless failure to be what the world demands.

Presently the teacher enters, *Herr Oberlehrer* Ballerstedt, the first of a series of more or less ridiculous figures who make up the teaching staff at Hanno's school. It seems that he was intended for the ministry, but turned to teaching instead for two reasons: he has a tendency to stutter and, as suggested by his round figure and sensuous face, a love for eating and drinking which he can indulge from private means. After obtaining a measure of quiet in the room, Ballerstedt calls upon young Perlemann to begin with the standard review, in this case, of the Book of Job. The scene unfolds with Mann's delightful understanding and sympathy for the agonies of boyhood, its incompetence to be what is called for, to deliver what is required.

We know that like the I O U's of Micawber or the vows of a Fat Abbot, the lessons will not be learned, the right performance will not be achieved; despite the terrifying formality of the world and its demands, human life in its pitiable units will go its halting way, declaring itself for what it is and cannot otherwise be, faulty and absurd. But luckily the lesson begins well with Perlemann offering a good summary in his quiet voice. The mood and tone of Monday morning seem inert, even somnolent, as recovery from the indulgences of Sunday comes slowly in, and the lads are hopeful that Perlemann may be allowed to drone softly on. But he is quickly released with a good mark, to make way for Heinricy.

We are soon aware that pupils are called only by their last names, an added note of formality and maturity which is incongruously belied by the weakness of those involved.

Heinricy now puts forth that classic of lame excuses: he was absent from the previous recitation. So the fearful accents of denunciation fall upon the culprit's ears. Heinricy is exposed as perpetually weak and incompetent—even worse, as bent on defending his inexcusable deficiencies, thus leaving no hope of elevation or betterment, of rising from his damnation to blessedness. The language employed is in ludicrous contrast to the boy's trivial offense: to his being little more than a child to begin with and so displaying the universal but harmless sinfulness of his time of life. A small, weak, and tender part of nature is taken for the whole in a passage of incongruous heaviness.

The indictment ends, Heinricy is ordered to his seat, and then "*Wasservogel, fahren Sie fort,*" returns us to the demand that a summary of the Book of Job is called for—the title of the lesson under review not being without its effect on our comic sense. Is not Wasservogel once more a perfect name, coming at just the right moment to clash in its homely reality on one hand, its meaning of waterbird on the other, with the pompous severity of the teacher himself?

Wasservogel's ears are prominent, his fingernails are closely bitten; his personal ugliness borders on the repulsive, but his recitation is praised for zealous effort when, having secretly propped the text behind the back of another student, he cheats his way to safety, seemingly unaware of the further clash between the religious nature of the subject and his unethical means of presenting it. After a brief inventory of Job's possessions by Gottlieb Kaszbaum, Ballerstedt relieves the atmosphere by offering a lecture of his own, but no one listens as the stupor intensifies in the hot room. Kai gives his attention to a volume of Poe, and Hanno's eyes grow dreamy amid this placid interlude.

The corridor bell concludes the session, which means that after recess Latin must be faced—even more formidable, abstract, and remote from success than religion if possible. The lines for memorization from Ovid are there—dark, inexorable, hopeless, and Hanno understands nothing of them. In desperation he begs for some last-minute aid from Adolph Todtenhaupt himself, when he shall be called upon.

In the school yard, Hanno and Kai have a turn about.

The place is superintended by a vain young fellow of foppish, self-consciously overdressed appearance, a Dr. Goldener, whose manner is somewhat laughable. In his vigilance, he seems constantly to expect something wrong, a deviation upon which he may then pounce with avidity. This tone of a wrath about to descend is powerfully kept by the school's director, Dr. Wulicke, whom Kai suddenly spies walking in his garden.

"Here comes God Almighty," "*der liebe Gott,*" says Kai, who has invented this secret nickname for the great man. This figure too strengthens our sense of an Old Testament standard of justice in the schoolroom and throughout the events of the day. All is under the command of God almighty, His fearsome instruments of anger and unappeasable will. We recognize as inevitable the appearance of Dr. Wulicke—a most terrifying figure whose divine wrath seems constantly threatening to visit itself upon the erroneous. His principles are listed with that awesome abstractness of German terminology, the very words themselves seeming to defy anyone to gainsay their rightness, or evade their power. Authority, duty, force, and service are now contrasted with the cheerful humanism of the school's former discipline, as the God of Israel prevails, equally terrible in laughter and in anger, totally unaware of incongruity in his capricious, arbitrary, self-willed behavior.

Dr. Wulicke's nickname of "*der liebe Gott*" being Kai's invention, unknown to the other students, helps to place the Count and Hanno more deeply in their own separate world. The two outcasts do not share the standard ridicule of their teachers heard among the others; they have created their own comic terms and attitudes, more detached and coolly ironic. Their special enmity toward the teachers and the school takes a far subtler, more imaginative form, understandable mainly to themselves with a kind of contemptuous aloofness. As Kai practices their special private mockery, Hanno is vastly amused and bursts out laughing as he is never seen to laugh at anything shared by the rest of his class.

Now the bell rings for the dreaded hour of Latin and the boys return to encounter *Oberlehrer Doktor* Mantelsack, who shares the faintly ridiculous aspect of all their teachers, suggested by one crude detail: Mantelsack and all the rest except the foppish Goldener wear their trousers too short. Mann's treatment of Sesemi Weichbrodt and Tony's other female teachers appears more tolerant than this succession of defective men, as if to say that women do not strike him as colored by a pompous incongruity that is typically masculine. But, aside from appearance, Mantelsack's peculiarity is that he selects favorites among the students who can do no wrong while they are in favor. The work of others is severely reviewed and they are chastised with red-ink annotations in one of those sinister dark books that act throughout the day as a symbolic record of behavior to be reviewed on the day of final judgment.

Meanwhile, Hanno in fear and trembling awaits the turn of those in the letter B. As Mantelsack utters the name Buddenbrook, however, he suddenly changes course and calls on a favorite of his, using the boy's first name as a mark of favor. Unluckily Edgar Lüders excuses himself from reciting by reason of illness: a bad headache prevented study. After scolding Lüders moderately, Mantelsack asks Timm to recite, and Hanno begins to relax, seeing that as long as no special alphabetical order is being followed he may easily escape notice entirely. Now Timm is almost caught looking at his text but, when Mantelsack comes down from the desk to investigate, Timm cleverly evades him by flattery: he is so excited and confused by the teacher's immediate presence that he cannot recite properly. Then as Mantelsack returns to his own place, Timm recovers the right page in his text. His fraud and pretense are rewarded by praise and absolution, which everyone, including Timm himself, considers to be just.

Again Hanno hears a name other than his own ring out, but Mumme, not expecting to be called on today, flounders badly and is denounced wrathfully as both stupid and lazy: a wretched figure, he sinks back into his seat in disgrace without extenuation. A small boy's venial offense is absurdly overwhelmed in language of awful power, and now the terrible moment comes at last for Hanno. He must rise when his name is called and he is about to make a desperate excuse when the boy in front of him, Hans Kilian, hands back the open text from which Hanno manages the pretense of a halting recitation, covered up by a poor reading of the Latin verse itself.

He seems like one struggling to recall, makes some errors and tries to conquer his aversion to the cheat he is guilty of by offering a generally mediocre recitation. Mantelsack is obliged to denounce Hanno for lack of rhythm, for his poor sense of the music of Ovid's verse. Unable to understand this from one who plays the piano, Mantelsack none the less records a fair mark as reward for effort. Like all the others, however, Hanno is by now convinced that Mantelsack is right, that he has in fact performed creditably after working hard. Yet he soon realizes that his only success was a fraud.

Now there follows an outright catastrophe as the next lad, Petersen, is accused of having a key to translation in his text. When the key is exposed and thereupon extracted from Ovid, long-suffering and much abused this day, the unhappy Petersen is denounced as the blemish of shame, "*der Schandfleck der Klasse.*" Once more the entire group accepts the disgrace of Petersen as deserved, just as the escape of Timm and Hanno is thought justified in their being shown as good students despite their having cheated as clearly as Petersen himself.

Alas, here as in the world success alone matters. If one prevails in love and war, who asks whether by force or fraud? Our little schoolboys too learn to see the world as it is, accepting its flagrant injustice, the contradiction throughout the day between profession and practice, with no sense of outrage. But as Hanno reflects upon the meaning of the world his eyes fill with abhorrence, terror, and denial—those eyes and their blue-tinted shadows toward which the comic tolerance of Mann begins inexorably to recede.

Hanno takes no joy in the good luck of his escape, which soon runs out in any case as chemistry under Dr. Marotzke exposes his own and Kai's ignorance, with the inevitable severe judgment recorded in the book of doom. There follows an hilarious hour in the class in English, presided over by Candidate Modersohn, the apprentice teacher. The fearful Old Testament austerity of preceding classes now gives way before a frantic riot of disorder, horseplay, bird calls, animal noises, and impudent misbehavior. A squinting caricature appears on the board, the door won't close, and as Modersohn comes in he steps on a toy torpedo, while his hand becomes soiled with ink as he places it on the desk. Amid the tumult he tries to call out various names, to be greeted by mockery and comic outcries of "missing," "dead" or "gone insane." This last joke was delivered by Kai in answer to Perlemann's name, and Hanno hugely amused begins to laugh. It is the last time we shall have laughter from our young friend, who will soon give way before a world in which he does not belong. Suddenly Modersohn betrays the enslaved cowardice of his soul by crying out a severe reprimand against Hanno for his misbehavior.

The boy now looks at the person and manner of Modersohn and sees beyond them to the man's impoverished meagreness of spirit, seeing why Modersohn singles him out as an easy object of tyranny simply because Hanno lacks the impudent loudness of the others. His last innocent merriment condemned by this representative of the world, Hanno must deny his pity to a thing so mean. The more or less harmless pomp and vain severity of the other teachers is lost in the sordid cheapness of this coward. The comic experience begins a final retreat into the shadows; incongruous absurdity becomes one with its opposite, laughter and sorrow grow blurred and indistinct one from the other.

Modersohn finally unearths someone who is neither dead nor insane and who takes up the recitation of English verse; but soon all pretense of order is lost and the wild horseplay is unconfined. A chicken crows, a pig grunts, and the dried peas go flying, a musical clock rings out "*Du, du, liegst mir im Herzen*" when suddenly the door flies wide open and "*der liebe Gott*" enters the room.

The transformation in behavior, sound, and appearance is instantaneous and absolute as an absurdly comic metamorphosis takes place in every person in the room. Nothing counts but power in this world, it would seem, and no one, including especially these young, respects anything else. In absolute silence the great man seats himself next to the wretched and trembling Modersohn; in a terrifying voice, a veritable "*Kontrabaszorgan,*" he bids the recitation continue. Amid the almost universal ignorance now disclosed, Modersohn's incompetence is revealed, his career ruined. Adolph Todtenhaupt, to be sure, and a few others might pass muster, including the young Count Mölln, whose accidental private interest in *Ivanhoe* prepares him to translate a fragment of this romance. But when called upon Hanno is a total failure, a fact inexorably recorded by God almighty in the fearful Doomsday class book, destroying all hopes of promotion at Easter time.

The bell at last rings to bring the hour to its close, and our young friends file out sadly into the school yard. Poor Kai struggles to console Hanno; he is sorry that he has made his friend seem inferior by knowing a little about *Ivanhoe*. But after all Hanno knew or seemed to know a bit of Latin, so that neither should feel betrayed by the other. Kai now delivers himself of a half-comic yet shrewd and bitter analysis of the teaching hierarchy and its titles, when the young require nothing more than a teacher who can in fact teach, but for whom the hierarchy provides no proper title. His conclusion is at once laughable and telling, despite the hopeless distance between his pitiable boyhood and the untouchable height of authority. Well, let them be, he says, nothing but a pack of rhinos, "*Nashörner*" as they are.

But Kai's energy and scornful defiance cannot prevail against the despairing mood of his dear young friend.

He is doomed in such a world as this, and now in a speech of terrible resignation and surrender Hanno reveals a tragic insight into his own fate. In the knowledge that his life can never come to anything, he declares his own death wish and so foretells his coming end.

Today he has still to endure geography under Dr. Mühsam, who visits a number of his choicest sarcasms upon Hanno, discovered in the act of looking over at Adolph Todtenhaupt's notebook. The last hour offers instruction and practice in drawing under Herr Drägemüller, a ludicrous figure and the victim of a number of droll eccentricities, among them a habit of changing from one wig to another depending on the length of his beard. Mann's comic invention is thus unflagging as the day nears its close with Kai working away at his new story and Hanno performing in imagination an orchestral overture—oblivious of the futile incoherence of Herr Drägemüller's discourse.

The long chapter ends with Hanno in the half-darkness at his piano, surrendering himself to one of his fantasies, healing the wounds of failure with music. His creator has seen the day in all of its incongruity, his inexhaustible comic invention exposing with disdain a parade of knavery, vanity, and hypocrisy, looking on with a kindly smile at harmless forms of human weakness, accepting at last with the greatest tenderness and pity his little hero's refusal of the call of life.

Index

The manuscript was edited by Ralph R. Busick and the book was designed by Peter Nothstein. The type face is Baskerville, originally designed by John Baskerville about 1790.

The book is printed on S. D. Warren's Olde Style Antique, white wove paper and bound in Columbia Mills' Riverside Chambray cloth over boards. Manufactured in the United States.

Bernard N. Schilling is Trevor Professor of English and Comparative Literature at the University of Rochester. He is also author of *Human Dignity and the Great Victorians* (1946), *Conservative England and the Case Against Voltaire* (1950), and *Dryden and the Conservative Myth* (1961).